MASON BEE REVOLUTION

MASON BEE REVOLUTION

2ND EDITION

How the Hardest Working Bee

CAN SAVE THE WORLD

One Backyard at a Time

DAVE HUNTER AND JILL LIGHTNER

SKIPSTONE

Published by Skipstone, an imprint of Mountaineers Books—an independent, nonprofit publisher
Skipstone and its colophon are registered trademarks of The Mountaineers organization.

Printed in China
29 28 27 26 1 2 3 4 5

Design: Jen Grable
Cover photographs, clockwise from top left: *A pollinator-friendly garden* (Pollinator Partnership.org); *Red mason bee* (Osmia rufa) *in nesting tube* (© getty/markhortonphotography); *Leafcutter bees using reeds* (Dave Hunter/Crown Bees); *Mason bee on rosemary* (Jennifer Bosvert/Shutterstock)
Back cover photographs, from top: *Flowers attract pollinators in vegetable gardens.* (Gina Lee Rodgers/Shutterstock); *Alfalfa leaf bees* (Dave Hunter/Crown Bees); *Raspberry crops will benefit from mason bee pollination.* (Jill Lightner)

Library of Congress Control Number: 2025944497

Printed on FSC®-certified materials

ISBN (paperback): 978-1-68051-710-1
ISBN (ebook): 978-1-68051-711-8

MIX
Paper | Supporting responsible forestry
FSC® C188448

Skipstone books may be purchased for corporate, educational, or other promotional sales, and our authors are available for a wide range of events. For information on special discounts or booking an author, contact our customer service at 800.553.4453 or mbooks@mountaineersbooks.org.

Skipstone
1001 SW Klickitat Way
Suite 201
Seattle, Washington 98134
206.223.6303
www.skipstonebooks.org
www.mountaineersbooks.org

LIVE LIFE. MAKE RIPPLES.

To Barb, my life partner and best friend. Love you.
–Dave

For Tom, because he's the bee's knees.
–Jill

CONTENTS

INTRODUCTION:

HOW SOLITARY BEES CAN SAVE OUR FOOD AND GARDENS

I (Dave) have been raising mason bees for almost 35 years. Over these decades, what was once my backyard hobby has grown into a business that supports gardeners, hobby orchardists, and commercial farmers in maintaining healthy habitats for mason and leaf bees and contributing to their population. These two species of solitary bee work alongside other wild or managed bees of all kinds as a cooperative addition to the entire range of agricultural production, from urban container gardens to large-scale orchards. These tiny pollinators are so effective at what they do that their impact on our harvests is undeniable—all in exchange for a small amount of human effort and a shift in our perspective about what it means to garden with pollinators in mind.

When I founded Crown Bees in 2008, my original goal was to raise mason bees for the almond industry. These bees, unlike social honey bees, do not live in hives; like many other solitary species, they are content to live side by side with others of their kind. This original project involved the coordination of more than 600 gardeners across northwest Washington, but things grew and changed along the way. In 2010, I launched Crownbees.com to help people learn to raise mason bees as successfully as possible, adding

More than 130 species of "hole-nesting" bees can nest in holes ranging in size from ⅛-inch to 5⁄16 inch. (Dave Hunter/Crown Bees)

leaf bees a few years later. A newsletter named *Bee-Mail* was launched, providing monthly tips on when to do what. My team and I researched and developed ethical products, with the goal of maintaining the health of these bees, while still being easy for humans to use. The following year, Crown Bees offered its line of products through nurseries, garden centers, and hardware stores. The first edition of this book was published in 2016; videos and US Department of Agriculture (USDA) research projects followed. There is no end to the interest people have in mason and leaf bees, or in the benefits that these two species can offer to the food supply. It is no small goal I have in mind: I want to assist with the world's pollination demands through the promotion of the human use of cavity-nesting bees (which includes mason and leaf bees), while supporting healthy, robust populations of pollinators everywhere.

When I first met the mason bee all those years ago, I didn't understand much about bees, let alone growing food. Like most young gardeners, I knew that if I did not water things they typically died. Keeping a green and tidy lawn was more important than growing native plants

CUTTING THE NAME TO "LEAF BEE"

Depending on where you live, you may refer to the *Armadillidiidae* family as pill bugs, potato bugs, or roly-polies. While most of North America calls a certain glowing insect a firefly, in scattered pockets of the US, they're known less elegantly as lightning bugs. The insect world is so extensive, and so present in our lives, that people give different groups of insects all sorts of different common names, including bees. Throughout this book, you'll see them called leaf bees, rather than leafcutter bees, even though their scientific name remains *Megachile rotundata*.

LEFT: *Leaf bees use leaves to close their nesting holes.* (Marc Sims/Shutterstock) RIGHT: *Male mason bee on rosemary* (Jennifer Bosvert/Shutterstock)

or food for my family. Although I did nothing to assist the bees, I was always grateful to harvest a few apples or plums from trees in the yard. Then one day my wife came home after visiting a friend and commented that this friend had significantly more apples than we did. I am an engineer by degree and needed to solve this puzzle.

It turned out that the friend was raising mason bees. All I had to do was put out a few blocks of wood with holes in them and the bees would do the rest. How simple! I bought a tube of mason bees from one of the few vendors I could find in the early 1990s and taped it next to my drilled blocks of wood. Midspring I walked past the nesting holes and found wild bees using them, yet the tube of bees had not opened. I peeled back the paper to find all of the bees I'd purchased had died. I had not needed to buy bees in my area—they were already there. Lucky me!

Through the years my fascination with these bees grew, as did the amount of fruit we harvested. Assisted by my kids, I learned how to harvest cocoons each fall from handmade wooden trays and keep the cocoons outside in a box. I remember one of my sons watching with awe as a little bee chewed its way out of the cocoon he was holding, only to fly away after sunning itself for a few minutes on his small hand.

Then, one stormy February afternoon, I found a few mason bee cocoons on the pavement where my teenage daughter parked her car. Bending close, I found about 10 percent of my several hundred cocoons stuck to the wet asphalt. The wind had blown over my unprotected box and scattered my years of steadily increasing bee numbers into the wild. I started over having learned a tough lesson: I needed to get serious about protecting my bees at every stage of their life cycle.

A wonderful thing happens to gardeners when they first introduce solitary bees into their gardens. Emotionally, it is much like owning a

Without pollination, this fruit would not exist. (Helgeson Orchard)

pet. The process starts with an attraction to their sheer cuteness or adorable personality. You bring your new companion home, and as the relationship develops, you pay careful attention to their particular needs—the quality of their food, a comfortable bed, a secure fence or satisfying scratching post. Then come important preventive medicines, behavioral training, and the maintenance of a safe living space, without poisonous snacks or plants lying within reach. You might even find that love triumphs over your initial intentions. No dogs on the bed? Good luck with that!

Likewise with your collection of solitary bees, whether you are primarily interested in mason bees for spring-flowering fruit trees or leaf bees for summer berries and vegetables. As you learn to care for them, you will begin to look beyond your fence, lawn, and landscaping. You will develop a specific motivation to care about one or two species of bee in particular rather than a vague concern for all bees everywhere. You'll fine-tune your gardening practices and add new plants with your bees' preferences as much in mind as your personal taste. Like your emotional connection with your pet, you'll realize that you've formed a bond with these useful and interesting insects, one that may go deeper than you would have ever predicted. Why should you be motivated to care for these bees? Read on—but be warned that it is sobering stuff.

POLLINATOR HEALTH IS CRITICAL

When we talk about pollinators, a basic fact often gets glossed over: *Pollination is fundamentally necessary for humanity's survival.* Aside from the wild, plant-filled habitats that sustain our oxygen, globally we cultivate approximately 1,400 types of plants. These produce all the land-based food and plant-based products we rely on, including cotton, hemp, bamboo, and flax for textiles as well as alfalfa for livestock feed. Of these 1,400 crops, nearly 80 percent depend on animals for pollination, encompassing a splendid variety of bee species plus bats, butterflies, birds, and moths. If these pollinators fail, so will we.

We are not talking about unusual, surprising, or easily replaceable foods either—this goes way beyond the deeply troubled almond industry, which has become something of a poster child in discussions of North American agricultural problems, from colony collapse disorder (CCD) to water usage, biodiversity, and drought concerns. Without thriving populations of all species of pollinators, we will lose apples, pears, cherries, peaches, plums, avocados, and most kinds of citrus as well as those popular almonds. Closer to the ground, we will lose pumpkins and other squash, melons, cucumbers, and all our delicious berries, including blueberries, raspberries, and cranberries. Canola and sunflower oils? Gone. The deciduous hardwood forests we rely on for wood? Greatly reduced, if not entirely vanished—those sturdy trees need pollination for their fertilization as much as our fruit trees and vegetables do.

The same dramatic weather events that impact humans also impact pollinators. Severe storms with high winds, drought, cold snaps in traditionally warm climates, and lingering wildfire smoke can be survivable, but less so when those coincide with the use of agricultural chemicals that are harmful to bees, the loss of their healthy wild habitat, and the parasites and diseases that can do great harm to specific bee species. In North America, we hear less about CCD than we used to, but the varroa destructor mite is still out there, spreading harm to multiple honey bee generations at once. There are also alarming new parasites, like the Houdini fly, first confirmed in the United States in 2011 and now spread across much of the continent.

For most of us in North America, it is less well known that the extensive wild bee die-off in China has led to farmers in some provinces painstakingly pollinating apple trees by hand over the last decade. China is the world's leading honey producer by far, with more than 8 million managed hives and an annual honey harvest of more than 460,000 metric tons (estimated as of 2022,[1] and more than twice the harvest of Turkey, which is in second place), yet the first deeply researched analysis of the health of its pollinator populations wasn't published until 2015. African honey-producing nations like Ethiopia, Tanzania, and Kenya have relatively healthy populations of honey bees, but as with other parts of the world, they struggle with pollinator-friendly habitat loss.[2] Chile, a large exporter of tree fruits and home to thriving honey and queen bee export industries, saw a huge drop in honey production in 2011, and there have been few signs of recovery, due at least in part to megadrought.[3] While the severity of declines varies around the globe due to myriad factors,

Most honey bees carry pollen on their hind legs with little falling off. (Photo courtesy Crown Bees)

these numbers show that problems with bees are not unique to the United States. In almost every instance, they point out that pollinators of all kinds, not only honey bees, are in peril.

These troubles are known to researchers and commercial farmers in individual countries, and generally their governments are also aware of problems and the resulting concerns over feeding their citizens as food prices rise. International panels of pollination experts have convened and issued lengthy reports. Nonetheless, little is being done to draw a connection between these massive challenges and the surprising potential that lies in everyone's home and community garden spaces.

RETHINKING THE HONEY BEE

The process of getting food on our tables is a more complex tapestry than you may understand. Well before you've made breakfast, your meal has been affected by climate, soil, water rights, farmworker expertise, and labor

BEES 101

- North America has approximately 4,000 bee species. There are small and large bees within this huge variety.
- Globally, there are seven bee families. This book is primarily concerned with Megachilidae (which includes solitary mason and leaf bees). The other two largest families are Apidae (which includes all species of bumble bee as well as honey bees) and Halictidae (an enormously diverse group often referred to as sweat bees).
- Solitary bees make up nearly 90 percent of the North American bee population.
- Social bees have changing duties in their six-week lifespan, while solitary bees each perform all jobs.
- Spring solitary bees overwinter as adults in cocoons; summer bees overwinter as larvae. Solitary bees emerge from their cocoons in response to a mix of specific outdoor temperature cues and a decrease in their fat reserves. Mason bees come out in the early spring, leaf bees later in the summer.
- Honey bees make honey. Few other bees do.
- Male bees cannot sting.
- All bees protect their egg chambers with specific natural materials they find nearby, including mud, leaf bits, tree resin, pebbles, cactus pulp, and saliva.
- An estimated 99 percent of flowers landed on by mason bees get pollinated—2,000 per day, versus about 15 per day for honey bees. This difference is because they carry their pollen differently.
- By providing wild bees with the food and habitat they need, you can attract them to your yard or patio containers.

availability. Researchers in academia, the government, and for-profit corporations have investigated new new problems, such as diseases, pests, and changes in climate as well as social issues such as shifting trends in our dining habits. Massive infrastructure is required to affordably move food from where it is grown to where people live. Don't forget the necessary packaging and all that goes into its production. These disparate and often hidden parts of the system have a role, just so you can enjoy your breakfast of coffee and an egg alongside a bowl of berries and yogurt. When examining problems in this process, we must fight our natural tendency to reach a quick conclusion about an issue and never investigate it again—we can't just make up our minds and leave it at that.

CCD provides an excellent case study of our tendency to seek simple, fast solutions when part of the farm-to-fork process is threatened. Thanks to extensive media coverage in the 2010s, problems with the bees that pollinate many large-scale agricultural crops are at least somewhat familiar to people who do not normally think much about the inner workings of our food supply. However, if you ask more casually informed people what they know about the disorder, they will say it has a single cause and often that the cause has been pinpointed. That could not be further from the truth.

Honey bees have always struggled with a number of threats: parasites like the varroa mite or *Nosema apis* fungus, diseases like the bacteria-based foulbrood or the fungal chalkbrood, and a wide assortment of viruses. More recently, honey bees have coped with huge varieties of pesticides, some of which are as toxic to them as breathing spray paint fumes is for humans. As research into CCD began, different studies seemed to point to each of these existing threats as the prime cause of the disorder, along with malnutrition, stress, climate change, hive management, genetically engineered crops, and radiation from cell phones. The cell phone issue at least has been officially debunked, but some 61 factors remain as causes of concern.

All these hypotheses added up to one reality: Researchers were not certain why colonies were disappearing in such massive numbers. Meanwhile, beekeepers in the United States have been reporting an annual loss of 20 to 30 percent of their hives for nearly two decades. North American beekeepers who transport their hives across state and province lines report anywhere from 30 to 90 percent annual die-offs; the die-off of stationary beehives hovers between 40 and 60 percent. According to the nonprofit Bee Informed Partnership, in the preliminary data for the 2022–2023 pollinator year, US beekeepers reported a collective hive loss of just over 48 percent.[4] At the time, this was the second-highest loss rate since 2010, but we should expect this record to be broken again and again.

Rates of loss vary across other continents, and many are not as bad as North America, but honey bees are not completely healthy anywhere. Thankfully, scientists are trained to rigorously question accepted wisdom, and new studies and papers are published with regularity. These days, many of the studies no longer focus on the broad issue of CCD but instead examine some of the more specific threats to the bees—a particular disease, a class of chemicals, a style of hive management, or the reasons a parasite can shift from being manageable by the bee's immune system to raging out of control. No single cause has yet been pinpointed for our massive pollinator die-off, but many pieces of data

Alfalfa leaf bees in a vegetable bed, female on the left, male on the right (Dave Hunter/Crown Bees)

are being produced that offer help to pollinators of all kinds in the short term.

ANCIENT PRACTICES, MODERN UNDERSTANDING

Humans understand that we cannot rely on a single crop for abundant food and correct nutrition. What we have been slower to realize is that we also cannot rely on a single pollinator. We tend to focus too heavily on one: the honey bee. A sustainable world depends on, and healthfully supports, many different pollinators, from solitary wasps to migratory butterflies and bats to the dozens of species of eye-catching bumble bees that populate their own little microclimates within North America.

Vegetable gardeners are often familiar with the concept of companion planting, notably the combination of corn, beans, and squash that the Haudenosaunee (Iroquois) grew in a no-till style now widely known as the Three Sisters (other Native peoples throughout North America have variations, depending on soil, water, and cultural practices). This idea is not limited to vegetables either. Clematis vines do better if their roots are shaded, for example, so a low-growing shrub in front of the flowering vine not only looks nice but keeps the vine healthier. Nasturtiums are so beloved by aphids that they can work to protect other plants, such as roses, from aphid damage; they sacrifice themselves in the process, but it keeps the roses in great shape. In contrast, the strong fragrances of rosemary and sage are capable of deterring a number of beetles from invading a vegetable patch. Even farmers who grow only one kind of fruit, such as cherries, will grow many different varietals to cross-pollinate and boost their yields as well as to extend the season in which they receive income and to hedge their bets, in case a specific variety is affected by an untimely cold snap or heat wave. A cherry cultivar that ripens a little earlier or a little later might successfully avoid damage from that brief spell of uncooperative weather.

Crop rotation is another technique that dates back centuries. At least one written record of its basics, from 1700 BCE, has survived, although practices have greatly advanced in the ensuing centuries. Today, crop rotation is a fundamental bit of soil science that both large-scale farmers and gardeners with small vegetable plots use to their advantage.

Polyculture (the planting of several species within the same space) and permaculture or regenerative agriculture (a broad plan of working with, rather than against, nature that can sequester carbon in soil disturbed for cultivation rather than left wild) are ways of expanding on the ideas of companion planting and crop rotation, stretching the concepts to use natural qualities from the plant and animal worlds in the best possible ways. While monoculture (picture thousands of acres of nothing but corn or almonds) is cheaper for massive farms because farmers need only one set of equipment, and labor is a large expense only during a few times of the year, polyculture can help farmers better cope with our changing climate and reduce the need for chemical fertilizers and herbicides. In many cases, regenerative, polyculture methods hold one of the keys to higher crop yields through naturally building healthier soil.

We will not see the end of monoculture farms anytime soon, and some specific plant diseases, particularly funguses, may require a cure that is only available through modern chemicals, but there is an increasing awareness both on farms and in university agriculture programs that many ancient, Indigenous, sustainable practices have tremendous value, both economically and environmentally.

A mason bee bringing mud to her nesting hole (Dave Hunter/Crown Bees)

TURNING THE TIDE

"Poly-pollination" is much like polycultural farming, in that it has begun thanks to a change in our thinking. It does not mean that one pollinator is the key to a successful harvest, but that pollinators function best when several kinds are working together throughout the course of a year. And if one species of bee is struggling, why not explore the possibilities offered by other pollinators?

Like our sensible cherry farmer's different varieties ripening at different times and offering different levels of resistance to diseases and climate shocks, different species of bee have their own most active seasons, require somewhat different conditions to thrive, and are designed to more easily stave off different kinds of threats. Beyond the realm of bees, every member of the world of pollinators is active in its own way, seeking different times of day, weather conditions, and kinds of plants for their own uniquely evolved reasons—they might all be in search of nectar and pollen, but some are specialists while others prefer to generalize.

Honey bee hives support tens of thousands of bees, and these numbers boost their effectiveness. They are moderately effective pollinators

A graceful cut by a leaf bee (Yuttana Joe/ Shutterstock)

with a remarkable flying range, and they stay active for a number of months throughout the year as they pack their hives with nectar and pollen. (You will not see exactly the same bee every day all season—each day, the queen lays roughly 1,500 eggs, and approximately the same number of bees die.) The mason bee has a longer lifespan (about 56 total weeks, although the large majority of that takes place within a cocoon) and sticks much closer to its home, but it is a truly exceptional springtime pollinator. Like the honey bee, it can be moved in its home to another location, making it a good choice for large-scale agriculture. Later in the growing season, as mason bees wind down their weeks of pollination, the leaf bee emerges at the right time to pollinate alfalfa and other legumes, key crops useful both as animal feed and plant-based protein sources. These mason and leaf bees' gentle nature makes them a natural starting point for gardeners interested in introducing managed pollinators to their yards to live and work alongside wild pollinators.

These two solitary bees have much smaller foraging areas than honey bees and are tremendously affected by their immediate environments. Are there enough flowers for them to find good pollen and nectar? Is there adequate mud, as well as the correct type of leaves? Is there protection from harmful pests such as the Houdini fly and hungry woodpeckers? Has the gardener done what is needed to help the bees survive to pollinate the flowers and vegetable blossoms in the small areas where these bees will spend their short lives? If you do your job well one year, you will end up with additional bees to share with friends and neighbors the following spring.

The simple act of creating a pollinator-centered outdoor space begins a journey toward greater collaboration, more food on the table, and positive change that goes far beyond your garden. Raising mason or leaf bees in a backyard—and perhaps sharing your bees with other gardeners, community garden spaces, or commercial food producers—will inspire you to rethink many of your gardening practices, centering the idea of a complete ecosystem where each plant and animal visitor plays an important role in achieving and maintaining a healthy balance. One garden at a time, and one bee at a time, actively thinking about not just our daily bread but our children's children's food supply and global health: It's a vision that can bring us together.

CHAPTER 1

WHY KEEP GENTLE BEES?

When people hear "beekeeping," they almost always picture honey beekeepers in helmeted spacesuits fretting over their hives for hours and might imagine the need to purchase heavy-duty equipment to get started. In reality, the options for home beekeeping are much wider. In the case of two species in particular, getting started is much simpler, and the annual maintenance requires little time.

SOCIAL VS SOLITARY

There are thousands of species of bees around the world, and approximately 4,000 are native to North America. A casual observer might divide them into four basic categories: honey bees, the ones requiring those goofy spacesuits for their keepers; wasps, which look straight out of an *Aliens* movie; hornets, who bother us at our picnics and can generate serious fear even in people who are not allergic to them; and bumble bees, the cartoonishly cute teddy bears of the bee world. The common belief is that all of these flying bugs live in families called hives and work together to build and maintain their home, collect and store food, and protect their queen.

YOU WON'T FEEL A THING, 'CAUSE THEY AIN'T GOT NO STING

While female mason and leaf bees are definitely capable of stinging, they are unlikely to do so; they did not evolve to have the more aggressive defensive attitude of social bees. Even if you went out of your way to get stung by grabbing one and giving it a squeeze, or accidentally stepped on one with your bare foot, the sting would typically be mild, like a pinprick, compared to the fierce discomfort of a social bee's sting. The gentlemen are even more polite: Male mason and leaf bees do not have stingers at all.

If you have a known, severe allergy to bee venom, it may be worthwhile to check with your doctor or an allergist who is familiar with solitary bee biology before keeping them, but understand that humans typically react much less to the amount of venom that solitary bees have.

The big surprise for that casual observer is that these social bee species make up only about 10 percent of all North American bees; the remaining majority are of a completely different type. These other thousands, both bees and wasps, are known as solitary.

The category of solitary bee encompasses many different habits—a simple example is that some prefer underground nests, while others like their homes higher up—but many are excellent pollinators. Of these solitary species, the mason bee is one of the first bees to appear in the spring (see Table 1.1), which means that your springtime garden will derive the benefit from its pollinating efforts. The name "mason bee" can refer to a number of different species, all of which are solitary. They are members of the *Osmia* genus, which can use either soil or material sourced from plants in their nests. Depending on where you live and how academic the discussion, in North America you might hear them called orchard mason bees, blue orchard bees, orchard bees, or simply mason bees. They are most likely one of two species: *Osmia lignaria* (blue orchard mason bee) or *Osmia cornifrons* (Japanese orchard bee).

The leaf bee, *Megachile rotundata*, is one of some 240 North American species in the *Megachile* genus, which use small bits of specific types of leaves for their nests. They need warmer weather than mason bees (see Table 1.1), making them useful for pollinating crops that blossom later in the year than the early flowers that appeal to mason bees. While they are also known as leafcutter bees, this casual name creates a mental image of highly destructive garden pests, such as snails, munching through foliage, which is not at all the case. For the purposes of this book, we'll call them mason and leaf bees.

LEFT: *A female mason bee with a dusting of pollen on her body* (Dave Hunter/Crown Bees) **RIGHT:** *Pollination in action by a leaf bee* (Bryan Reynolds)

While there are key differences between the two, they have many similarities.

UNDERSTANDING DIFFERENCES IN BEE-HAVIOR

Social bees and wasps are extraordinarily hierarchical. Sort of like the different classes of people in Aldous Huxley's *Brave New World*, every insect has a specific role to play throughout its life. With honey bees, each worker will live for about six weeks, performing a variety of duties, including forager; scout; nurse bee; hive guard; nectar, pollen, or water collector; or queen attendant. None of the workers will reproduce. The queen is the sole reproductive member of a hive, and her lifespan varies by species—a year is common, while some live as long as five years.

All social insects share a home with a common entrance, whether that home is a paper nest, a hole in the ground, or an artificial hive. Except for a few stingless bee species native to tropical or subtropical regions, guard bees will defend their home and their queen by stinging, which can make them seem aggressive. Social bees' shared mentality is referred to as "hive mind," and it is particularly evident during a swarm, when a queen leaves the hive under the protection of a large mass of worker bees. If you ever see this happen (swarms can appear in some fairly startling places, including the side of a car), do not call a pest removal service. Instead, contact a local honey company, apiary service, or beekeeping club so the hive may be given a new home.

In most respects, solitary bees could not be more different from social bees. For them, the hive mind does not come into play at all. While about 40 percent of solitary bees are female, each one is a reproductive queen, taking care of her own food, water, and nesting needs during her lifespan. Unlike social queens, the active, airborne life of a solitary queen is four to six weeks. Instead of sharing a nest with others of her species, each queen "owns" her own nesting holes. She may use several holes during a

TABLE 1-1
SOME COMMON POLLINATORS

BEES

SPECIES/FAMILY	COMMUNITY TYPE	ACTIVE MONTHS	TERRITORIAL PRESENCE
EUROPEAN HONEY BEE	Social	From first blossoming to September	Introduced across US and Canada
AFRICANIZED HONEY BEE	Social	From first blossoming to September	Introduced and confirmed in 9 states as of 2024; slowly spreading north
BUMBLE BEE	Social	Appears according to bloom of preferred flower, generally March–October	Native to US and Canada (46 species)
MASON BEE	Solitary	February–May	Primarily native to US and Canada (130+ species)
LEAF BEE	Solitary	June–September	Native to US and Canada (240+ species)
CARPENTER BEE	Solitary	June–September	Native to US and Canada (28 species)
DIGGER BEE	Solitary	June–September	Native to US and Canada (21 species)
MINING BEE	Solitary	May–August	Native to US and Canada (500+ species)

WASPS

SPECIES/FAMILY	COMMUNITY TYPE	ACTIVE MONTHS	TERRITORIAL PRESENCE
YELLOWJACKET WASP	Social	April–September	Both native and introduced to US and Canada
EUROPEAN WASP	Social	April–September	Introduced across US and Canada
PAPER WASP	Social	April–September	22 species in US and Canada
MUD DAUBER WASP	Solitary	June–September	30 species in US and Canada
POTTER WASP	Solitary	June–September	40+ species in US and Canada
POLLEN WASP	Solitary	May–August	14 species in US and Canada

PREFERRED LANDSCAPE	NEST TYPE	IDENTIFYING CHARACTERISTICS
Abundant flowering plants	Artificial hives, rock crevices, hollow trees	Slightly fuzzy, golden-striped bodies
Warm climate is key	Flat, vertical layers of walls; suspended from trees or walls	Smaller and darker than European honey bees; quick to swarm and attack if threatened
Large variety of flowers	Existing hole in the ground, birdhouses, or wherever a queen can find a safe, dry hole for her nest	Fat, fuzzy bodies with varying numbers of stripes; occasional defensive stings
Fruit or nut trees with nesting material nearby	Small holes to seal with materials such as mud, resin, pebbles, and cactus pulp	Dark, metallic bodies or brown with stripes
Meadows or vegetable gardens with thin, delicate leaves nearby	Small holes to seal with leaves	Small with black and ivory stripes
Warm, humid areas near abundant flowering plants	Channels drilled into soft wood	Dark, shiny, up to 1" (2.5 cm) long; somewhat clumsy
Near asters, in arid areas	Sandy, pebbly ground and cliffsides	Smooth abdomens with slight fuzz, black with pale stripes
Meadows, or lawns with fruit trees and flowers	Narrow channels underground or in sandy cliffsides	Black, dull metallic blue, or green with bands of pale hair on abdomen
Orchards, parks, picnic areas	Tree stumps or wooden eaves of buildings	Smooth, straight, yellow-and-black bodies; some with red and yellow stripes
Orchards, parks, picnic areas	Bulbous paper nests	Smooth, black-and-yellow-striped body with 3 dots on face; aggressive behavior
In or near forested areas	Open combs of paper; likes building in birdhouses	Narrow abdomens, brown and yellow stripes, less aggressive
Nectar-producing flowers with plentiful spider populations	Mud tubes that are entirely visible	Delicate bodies, mainly black; preys on spiders
Nectar-producing flowers with plentiful caterpillar populations	Small, jug-shaped bulbs attached to walls or trees	Shiny, delicate bodies, mainly black
Desert regions	Clusters of open mud cells attached to twigs	Like yellowjackets, but with noticeably clubbed antennae

THE NORTHERN GIANT HORNET

In fall 2020, this newcomer to North America made headlines as the "murder hornet," boosted by seemingly endless headlines, memes, and jokes. Researchers found it first in 2019, on both sides of the US-Canada border in the Pacific Northwest; additional nests were found and removed in 2020 and 2021. Naturally found in northern India and several Asian countries, these sizable insects (averaging 2 inches [5 centimeters] in length) are known to attack the nests of other hive-dwelling insects by decapitating all inhabitants, leading to scientific concern over how they could impact key pollinators if allowed to spread. Happily, no nests were found in 2022, 2023, or 2024, so researchers were able to declare this hornet officially eradicated in North America, while using their infamy to bring some attention to additional invasive insects such as the spotted lanternfly in the eastern United States.

season, depending on her species and how many eggs she lays.

Solitary bees do not make honey, and only a few species produce small amounts of beeswax—nothing that is harvestable. Regardless, mason and leaf bees are such exceptional pollinators that their lack of honey production is easy to forgive.

DIFFERENT WAYS OF BEE-ING

Honey bees and bumble bees are designed to tidily capture pollen to bring back to their nests. They are so focused on this job, and so efficient at packing the pollen into a body part called a *pollen basket*, that little is dropped. It's fairly easy to spot with the naked eye bright orange, full pollen baskets on bumble bees, and you may even see them methodically tucking pollen away on one flower before heading off to the next. Pollination is fairly accidental with these species, only occurring when they are sloppy at their work or have overloaded their pollen baskets.

Mason and leaf bees, meanwhile, also want to carry pollen back to their nests, but they collect it loosely on their fuzzy bodies, where the pollen has a tendency to drop off the fuzz as easily as it came aboard. To collect it, a bee will crawl slowly all over a blossom, gathering pollen and dropping it again as she flies erratically from flower to flower. It is probably a good thing mason bees are solitary, as they would be tremendously sloppy coworkers in the hive compared with the oh-so-efficient honey bee, but their fuzzy bellies and here-and-there flying habits make mason and leaf bees exceptional pollinators.

A single mason bee can pollinate enough cherry blossoms to net 12 pounds (5.4 kilograms) of fresh cherries. In comparison, a cherry orchardist needs 60 honey bees for the same size harvest. Scale up to a small commercial orchard of 50 trees, and the mason bee provides a remarkable benefit to the orchardist. Its dry pollen-carrying technique gets more blossoms pollinated, making it an ideal addition to any orchard. Meanwhile, the leaf bee so excels at boosting the alfalfa harvest that it has played a key role in its pollination since it was introduced from southwestern Europe in the late 1930s. As long as alfalfa is grown for animal feed, this bee should continue to see robust usage in the commercial realm.

Honey bees do offer some basic advantages over mason bees for commercial farmers. They come with their houses, so orchardists who lease them do not have to invest in and maintain bee boxes. Honey bees also travel with their own food supply, which means they can be brought into an orchard right before the blossoms open—they are ready and waiting in position for the starting gun to fire, so to speak. Another issue is that the chemicals that orchardists might be spraying on trees have likely been tested for safety on honey bees but not necessarily any other kind of bee (see chapter 5 for more detail).

WHY SO BUSY, BEES?

Honey bees are avid collectors of pollen, accumulating between 60 and 100 pounds (27–45.4 kilograms) of it per hive per year. The key difference with mason and leaf bees is in the word *collect*. Honey bees are not merely gathering food for a few eggs like our solitary bee friends. The honey bees that collect pollen must feed not only the hive's young but also its non-pollen-collecting adults, adding up to several thousand pea-sized mounds of nectar and pollen every day. Mason and leaf bees can afford to be more scattered in their pollen collection because they need so much less of it.

Honey bee hives are fascinating systems, but the hyperproductivity of a healthy hive is part of the reason that their keepers end the pollinating season with bee-made products they can use or sell. These products include beeswax, royal jelly (a milky substance used in skincare), and propolis (a resin used in supplements), in addition to honey. Because these all earn a relatively high

TOP: *Honeybees and bumblebees have pollen baskets, which neatly collect pollen to take back to the hive. Mason bees are less fastidious.* (lkordela/Shutterstock)
BOTTOM: *An apple blossom is an easy place to find both pollen and nectar for visiting bees.* (Dave Hunter/Crown Bees)

price per pound for a small farmer keeping their own bees, there is an obvious appeal. But a large agricultural operation will likely prefer to hire the honey bee pollinator service that offers a good price and is available when needed.

POLLEN'S PLACE IN THE GARDEN

Most of us are not serious orchardists. Perhaps you have a fruit tree or some berry bushes, or you have been thinking about adding one or the other to your garden. Perhaps your entire garden is grown in pots on an urban balcony or in a raised bed on the roof of your apartment building. Depending on what you have, you might think your pollination needs are already met, because many fruit trees and berry bushes sold today are labeled "self-pollinating." This phrase leads to the assumption that they do not need pollinating insects to help them along. This is an unfortunate misunderstanding, as only about 10 percent of plants are wind pollinated, needing no assistance from insects or, less commonly, birds.

What *self-pollinating* refers to is this: Originally, many kinds of berries and fruiting trees required two plants—one male and one female—to convert their flowers into any fruit at all. Farmers relied on the wind and wild pollinators to transfer pollen back and forth between the flowers, and only female plants would ultimately bear fruit. *Self-pollinating* means you do not need to worry about male and female plants, but pollen still needs to move between the blossoms on your tree or shrub. That is why encouraging effective pollinators in your garden can make a big difference.

Mason and leaf bees are so dedicated to crawling across flowers that much of the pollen dropping off their furry bellies lands right where you want it: on another nearby flower. When the wind drops pollen, it is as likely to blow down the street (directly into the face of an allergy sufferer) as it is to land on another part of your fruit tree. More pollen in the right place equals a greater chance of flowers becoming fruit.

If you ever have the opportunity to see a mason or leaf bee work side by side with a honey bee, you will spot a fundamental behavioral difference. Honey bees are extraordinarily methodical creatures. They begin work on one limb of a tree, collect pollen only from the blossoms on that limb until their pollen baskets are full, and then return to the hive. On their second trip to the tree, they will pick up near where they left off. They are so thorough that the process is sometimes referred to as "stripping the pollen." In comparison, mason bees look like distracted little grazers, flitting from a blossom on one tree to another blossom on a totally different tree. While you can imagine a honey bee frowning on and tsk-tsking this distracted behavior, mason bees are dropping pollen everywhere with this method, and it is terrific for cross-pollination.

A BIG ROLE FOR MASON BEES

Mason and leaf bees may not offer the high-value end products that honey bees do, but they are mighty capable of contributing to our food supply by pollinating as well as they do without any hive-centered hazards. In recent years, there have been semitruck crashes in Florida, Washington state, California's Death Valley, Ontario, and Idaho that share a specific detail: They have been carrying honey bee hives, which spilled millions of bees across the roadway. In many instances, not a single hive was rescued. While these collisions rarely happen on urban highways, they are frustratingly common. Aside from the loss of apian life in these crashes, the bees must contend with viruses, mites, beetles, chemicals, and funguses present in the environment in which they land.

Our heavy reliance on the honey bee and its myriad modern health issues has led to over 90 percent of the funding for pollinator research going toward this species' problems. Spreading our pollination needs and our agricultural research efforts across species, rather than focusing on only the honey bee, benefits everyone involved.

You don't need a yard to be a successful keeper of gentle bees. (Dave Hunter/Crown Bees)

A GLIMPSE AT MASON BEE SCIENCE

Modern research on mason bees dates back to 1957, when Dr. Marshall D. Levin and M. H. Haydak published a paper that examined different types of pollen and their relative nutritive values to this species of bee.[1] Levin was a leader in bee research at the USDA for 36 years and served as director of the Carl Hayden Bee Research Center in Tucson, Arizona, in the early 1960s. In 1967, he urged Arizona beekeepers to discontinue their use of the insecticide carbaryl, which was being used to target the damaging pink bollworm. As part of that warning, he noted that he had seen the number of Arizona's honey bee colonies drop from nearly 90,000 to fewer than 20,000 over a few years. It is disheartening to consider how much better off all our bees might be today if only this call to action had been heeded more widely. In the early 1970s, Levin became the USDA's national program leader for crop pollination and bees. Given his career, it is no wonder that nearly every research paper on mason bees written since then has used his early work as a reference.

Nearly four decades after Levin and Haydak's original paper, a fascinating study[2] was published by the team of Jordi Bosch, William P. Kemp, and Glen E. Trostle. After looking at nearly a decade of work with European mason bees (a cousin to North American mason bees) in orchards, they concluded three major points: First, mason bees prefer foraging on fruit trees. Second, this preference coupled with their short foraging range, makes it easy for farmers to concentrate their efforts right where they are wanted most. Third, mason bees are less picky about temperature or sunlight, so they are willing to work when it is cooler or darker; this gives them many more hours to pollinate than most other bees. The researchers were even able to do a direct comparison with honey bees, and the time difference was astonishing: Over five days, European mason bees spent more than 33 hours foraging for pollen in an apple orchard, compared with about 15 hours for honey bees. Honey bees turned out to be slackers!

Bees don't respect property lines and will happily pollinate fruit in a next-door neighbor's yard. (Jill Lightner)

Mason bees' close and dedicated contact with all the reproductive parts of the flower makes them incredibly effective pollinators of fruit tree blossoms.

Another fascinating argument in favor of supporting as many species of bee as possible was published online in early 2013 by the Royal Society. Authored by Claire Brittain, Neal Williams, Claire Kremen, and Alexandra-Maria Klein, it looked specifically at California's troubled almond orchards and concluded that honey bees are more effective when working side by side with other bee species, including mason bees.[3] When bees are more effective, the result is more fruit—in this case, more almonds.

The study provided a strong voice in favor of diverse ecosystems in agriculture. Studies in multiple regions[4] have found evidence that honey bees react to native bee competition by speeding up their pollen collection, a personality trait that can lead to problems with pollen availability for wild bees if there are too many honey bees around. From cherries to apples to almonds, research is showing that mason bees can make a big difference to commercial growers. While consumer education efforts and city regulations on landscaping chemicals are doing what they can to help the honey bee, and researchers are hard at work tackling their numerous problems, mason bees are a key species that almost everyone can support.

MORE BEES = MORE FOOD

All this is interesting stuff, but chances are you are not a cherry or almond farmer. You probably already see a smattering of honey bees and bumble bees visiting your yard each summer as it is. Perhaps you already have stopped using chemical treatments on your lawn and buy organic produce when you shop—why do more? There are a few compelling reasons, each with an altruistic side as well as a component of pure self-interest.

This is big-picture, long-term thinking. Because of the numerous challenges to the honey bee, every state has already seen a decline in this key pollinator. Thanks to commercial spraying to control pests on agricultural land, in suburban parks, and along urban streets in some regions, as well as diverse issues stemming from climate change, many wild bee species are also in trouble. Mason and leaf bee populations are hanging in there on their own, but without some thoughtful attention, their populations will not grow enough to compensate for pollinator losses in other areas. They can also be affected by regional use of pesticides, although they can be affected by slightly different ones than honey bees.

You can help increase wild mason or leaf bee populations by adding a bee house to your garden or a nearby community garden and then maintaining it annually to ensure pests are not decimating your bee house populations. Increasing the bees' numbers directly assists in increasing the yields of nearby fruit trees and summer vegetables. As you assist in increasing their total population, you will be expanding the good that pollinators do for food yields, boosting the fresh food supply at a modest level for your community.

PUTTING BEES FIRST = FEWER CHEMICALS

This is community-based thinking. A wide range of pesticides are being continually investigated for their effects on both honey bee health and human health. At the same time, herbicide companies are continually revising their sprays as weeds evolve to resist them. It's a race that nobody wins, and many species in nature have much to lose.

In the mid-20th century, these modern agricultural chemicals were seen as an elegant, scientific solution to a number of serious problems facing commercial food production: The 1970s and 1980s saw massive crop failures on many continents. The United States was able to quickly ramp up food production in part because of these chemicals, along with newly patented, high-yielding plant varietals that in many cases were also developed to withstand the increased use of pesticides. Techniques such as monoculture became the standard in large-scale agriculture in this era, because growing massive fields of a single crop makes it efficient to plant, grow, and harvest with

ALONE, BUT NOT LONELY

While they are definitely solitary bees (this means that every female is a queen), many mason and leaf bees are happy to live in the bee equivalent of a building full of studio apartments. They have no objection to sharing a bee house with plenty of neighbors, just as humans can enjoy living in dense urban neighborhoods. Each queen will choose her own nesting tubes within the bee house, just as we would each have our own apartment within a building. Each species has slightly different preferences for their homes and nearby plants as well as a different season of activity. It is possible to keep both types of bees (even in small gardens) or only one of them if you have a narrow garden focus.

A chemical-free garden with many different pollinator-friendly blooms (Pollinator Partnership.org)

minimal workers. Weeds could be eliminated through sprays that made farming much easier.

But we are now seeing many downsides to the agricultural practices of those decades, and smaller-scale organic, biodynamic, and regenerative farming techniques are being eyed as the right direction for many reasons. Washington State University was the first university in the nation to offer an undergraduate degree in organic agriculture, back in 2008; countless more from Florida to Michigan now offer it as an area of concentration or a postgraduate degree or have developed an undergraduate program in the looser arena of sustainable agriculture. What was once a topic reserved for hippies has become global agricultural curricula.

This shift in thinking is also seen in governments at many levels and in many places. Some city councils have moved to ban the spraying of public trees when they are in bloom or have acted to prevent the use of certain chemicals on government-owned land. In the European Union, three neonicotinoids have been banned for all outdoor use, and there are many North American resident activists trying to expand those bans. Consumers are also playing a role—after major hardware chains came under fire for selling nursery plants that had been treated with potentially pollinator-harming chemicals, some hardware chains announced they would phase out plants that had been treated with these chemicals. Unfortunately, without actual regulations, those announcements mainly amounted to meaningless PR campaigns.

Organophosphates are another broad category of chemicals coming under fire in the

United States and abroad. (Refer to chapter 5 for a list of specific chemical names that lurk within the neonicotinoid category and an overview of safer choices.) These efforts are scattershot, having bigger impacts in some communities than others, but nonetheless, change is happening.

You can be part of that friendly revolution by introducing mason and leaf bees into your own garden and treating them as a highly valuable addition, just as you would treat an expensive new plant. Gardening with bees in mind means reducing your own use of chemicals, and either finding natural treatments for plant diseases or learning to live with less-than-perfect aesthetics. A thriving ecosystem is within the reach of every gardener, whether you have only a tiny townhouse plot, a large suburban lot, or several acres all to yourself.

Putting bees first also means that you will expose yourself and your family to fewer potentially toxic chemicals while creating a thriving habitat for songbirds and pollinators.

SOLITARY BEES ARE COOL

Gardeners have their own reasons for the work they put into their yards. Novelist and poet Alice Walker once wrote about succumbing to a seasonal disease she termed "hollyhockitis," while single-topic books, clubs, and thriving societies relating to species as diverse as tea roses, tulips, dahlias, rhododendrons, moss, and native plants show that humans are capable of falling in love with almost anything that grows.

If you love a garden space, whether it is your own or it belongs to a family member or a community group, introducing mason or leaf bees is a worthwhile action that can improve that garden's long-term sustainability and short-term yields. Gentle mason and leaf bees are some of the best possible additions to your plant care routine, particularly when you grow any sort of fruit or vegetable intended for human consumption. They are fascinating little creatures that barely notice people as they move from flower to flower, and back to their home, repeating this busy work all day long.

A close look at the beautiful eyes of a male leaf bee
(Dave Hunter/Crown Bees)

At a glance, mason bees might look more like houseflies than bees—they are about the same size (females a bit bigger, males a bit smaller) as an average fly and have black bodies with pretty, dark blue-green iridescence. Unlike flies, they are visibly fuzzy, with beelike antennae and eyes and four wings, not two. If you pay close attention, you can spot the males by the white fuzz on their heads and longer antennae.

Leaf bees are smaller than mason bees and nest in smaller holes; their size is one of the qualities that make them such able pollinators of vegetables with small or narrow blossoms. While their general appearance is black, they have thin yellow-white stripes on their furry abdomens, like petite bumble bees. Look carefully and you will spot their antennae and four tiny wings. The males have beautiful iridescent green eyes.

These bees make a fantastic topic of conversation too. Many people have never heard of them, and what gardener does not love having the chance to teach friends and neighbors about the newest addition to their yard? These bees are gentle enough that they could be the subject of a child's science fair exhibit, sure to knock the socks off any teacher if your child is willing to put in the observation time.

Whether you keep them yourself, buy a starter kit as a housewarming gift for a friend, or bring supplies to your community's shared gardening space, mason and leaf bees need only a few key things to help them thrive.

Mason bee cocoon separation in a reed. Note the thick mud plug on the bottom at the entrance to the reed. (Dave Hunter/Crown Bees)

THE LIFE CYCLES OF MASON AND LEAF BEES

Introducing solitary bees to your garden is about as low maintenance an addition as it is possible to make. All told, a house of springtime mason or summer leaf bees requires about two hours of care over the course of a year. It is possible to spend more time than that merely pruning a rose garden!

The lifespan of both mason bees and leaf bees is about four to six weeks, and they do not venture more than a few hundred feet from where they emerged. The males emerge first, followed by females a few days later. They mate, and the ladies get to work immediately, collecting food in the form of pollen with a bit of nectar and placing it in the back of an available hole. Pollen, nectar, and their own saliva get kneaded into balls, and once the balls are the right size, an egg is laid on top of this mass of nourishment, which is called bee bread. Mason bees seal off the egg and its food with a delicate wall of mud, while leaf bees use tiny snippets of thin, sturdy leaves (like those from bean plants or lilac trees) in place of mud. Once the egg's cell is complete, the solitary queen returns to her pollen and nectar gathering, repeating the process for additional eggs. The nesting hole will ultimately contain between five and eight mason bee egg cells, or 10 to 15 for smaller leaf bees. The nesting tube entrance will then be sealed off, with either a slightly thicker layer of mud or leaf snips.

The next few months are somewhat different for the respective species: Mason bee eggs become larvae, which hatch, grow, and create delicate-looking but remarkably sturdy egg cocoons, ready to emerge as adults the following spring and repeat the cycle. Meanwhile, leaf bees overwinter in their cocoons as pupae and develop into adult bees once the weather warms up.

The order in which the eggs are laid shows a fascinating result of evolution. Male bees need to hatch first to be available when the more crucial females hatch. Males are, sorry to say, somewhat more expendable in terms of the overall survival of the species. According to the US Forest Service and North Carolina Extension Services, when the queens of these two solitary bee species fill their nest holes with eggs, female eggs (these were fertilized by sperm gathered when mating) are laid first, at the back of the nesting hole, and the males, from unfertilized eggs, are laid toward the front of the nesting hole. It is easier for them to hatch correctly when laid in this order. The males also happen to be on the front line in case a bird or similar predator finds the nest and decides it is interested in a snack of bee larvae.

With no hive to defend, each solitary bee works only for herself and her progeny; they are perfectly content to buzz happily past people, and they are so interested in pollen and nesting material that they do not act like pests during outdoor picnics or barbecues. Unlike honey bees, they do not swarm or behave in a territorial fashion. And because they stay so close to home, you know that the mason bees you have invested in will not spend their time pollinating a garden several miles from yours; at most, they will visit the gardens of your immediate neighbors if you have a small yard. By comparison, honey bees might fly across town in search of their perfect flowers.

Having your bees stick close to home also means that you are better able to control their exposure to unhealthy chemicals. If you do not use those chemicals (and you are comfortable encouraging your neighbors not to either), chances are the bees will not come in contact with them. This includes downright harmful sprays as well as nonorganic materials like chemical-based potting soils or turf builders that promise bumper crops and limited weeds. With your attention in cleaning the bee house and sorting cocoons each year, your bees are also less likely to be seriously harmed by parasites. There is zero concern about CCD—no colony means no collapse. All in all, they are easy to manage and offer remarkable benefits to your garden.

In terms of gardens or garden space, your plant varieties and garden chemical use are more important than the actual square footage. If you are primarily concerned with fruit trees, mason bees will be your bee of interest. You don't have fruit trees, but you'd like to boost pollination in your summer vegetable beds? The leaf bee is the right bee for you. If you have both fruit trees and warmer weather food crops, you can of course raise both species. Solitary bees can thrive happily in dense urban neighborhoods, as long as you can set them up for success with the right habitat. If that habitat involves an apple tree or patio containers loaded with cherry tomatoes at your next-door neighbor's, while you focus on providing a clean bee house and the correct nesting material, the bees won't mind a bit.

CHAPTER 2

PREPARING FOR SUCCESS WITH BEES

For people, yards and gardens are something to enjoy sporadically. Of course we want our plants to be healthy and for our outdoor space to have visual appeal, but the longest amount of time we are likely to spend in a yard is a long summer day. In contrast, bees make the outdoors their home 24/7, and it should be the source for everything they need to thrive. When you choose a new place to live, you might consider things like the attractiveness of the design, the quality of schools, the commuting time to your job, walkability, and available conveniences like libraries, grocery stores, and restaurants. Bees have their own wish lists, consisting of simple things that make one yard a more desirable place to live than another.

What might look like a green oasis to a human is, for a bee, the problematic neighborhood where you would never choose to settle down and raise a family: There's a broad moss- and clover-free lawn, kept that way through the application of chemical fertilizers and herbicides. The edges of the lawn might be framed by a heavy layer of gravel or bark to suppress weeds,

A variety of native flowers blooming from spring to fall will attract and feed your region's pollinators. (Pollinator Partnership.org)

along with mess-free trees (no fruit, minimal flowers) and modern hybrid flowering plants that look pretty and fit nicely in containers but do not offer much in the way of pollen or nectar. Invasive insects like aphids or caterpillars are dealt with by more chemicals, this time in the form of insecticides. Everything is controlled for the visual preferences of the gardener, with no consideration for how unbalanced this ecosystem has become through human intervention. Such gardens are all too common in our communities, and for our friendly pollinators, they are downright toxic. Making your outdoor space a "good neighborhood" may require rethinking your plant choices, your gardening practices, or both.

MASON BEES FIND JOY IN MUDVILLE

When a mason bee is looking for a home, she is in search of healthy sources of pollen, from bee-friendly herbs and heirloom flowers to blossoming trees that have not been sprayed with insecticides or fungicides. Just as you do not want to drive 10 miles to the nearest grocery store, she likes her food nearby—within 300 feet (100 meters) of her home. She prefers a nice hit of morning sun to wake her up early in the day with a warm and cozy house. At the same time, she appreciates a bit of shade to protect her from the hottest part of the day, since she cannot turn on a fan like we can.

Perhaps most appealing to her—and often the hardest for humans to come to terms with—is the necessity of a finely textured, nicely damp, silt- and clay-filled mud patch. Mason bees spend their days like dedicated DIY homeowners, always working on a new project. Like human masons need a steady supply of bricks and mortar to ply their craft, mason bees need continual access to the raw materials essential to

FIVE BEGINNING STEPS TO CREATING A BEE HAVEN

If you currently rely on chemical herbicides and pesticides for your garden's success, or you grow a traditional green lawn with minimal other attractions, these low-commitment steps will move you toward a more bee-friendly style of gardening.

1. **Add one native plant.** Species that belong in the habitat where you live tend to be easy to care for and have an already-existing beneficial relationship with your climate and its other native plants and animals. See our list of "Top 10 Native Plants for Pollinators in Seven Regions" for suggestions, later in this chapter.
2. **Grow one kind of food.** Tomatoes or herbs in containers are an easy place to start, but a fruit tree or berry bushes can be remarkably low maintenance as well as delicious and an enjoyable experience for young children. Choose something you love that suits your climate.
3. **Eliminate one pesticide, herbicide, or chemical fertilizer.** This might be an easy switch, such as enriching your garden beds with a fall application of compost instead of powdered fertilizer. If you are heavily reliant on routine applications of pesticides, you might have to broaden your horizons and relax your standards of appearance for a year while beneficial insects return to your yard, re-creating a natural ecosystem and beginning their work of keeping pests naturally in balance. You can also reduce environmental harm by switching to solutions like dish soap for aphids, or homemade milk sprays to replace heavy-duty fungicides. (See page 103)
4. **Allow one pest to live.** Some are more frustrating than others, but the presence of a pest might attract beneficial insects that will gobble the pest up without your direct involvement. From small mammals like a soil-aerating mole all the way down to beetles, snails, and aphids, learning to live with one might not be as painful as you think.
5. **Set up a mason or leaf bee house in your yard, balcony, or rooftop garden.** Now that you have made your environment more bee friendly, it is easy to set up a small house for these gentle bees. If you already have one at your home and a new neighbor moves in, bee houses and bees can be a fun housewarming gift.

their home building, as each egg will need to be protected by a thin layer of clay. This does not mean converting half of your yard to a mud pit—it is much easier and more subtle than that. But mud is a critical amenity for a mason bee neighborhood.

A mason bee mines the perfect mud for her nesting hole. (Dave Hunter/ Crown Bees)

What's the big deal with mud? Especially if you are a gardener with plenty of vegetable beds and minimal grass, you might feel like you have this covered. Please, think again! The right kind, and amount, of clay-rich mud is one of the most important things you can supply for your mud-using bees. And fair warning: They are picky about it in ways that are not immediately apparent to most of us—after all, mud is mud, right?

Not for mason bees. Moist, clay-rich soil is one of the primary materials they use to build their nests, and it is as important to them as it is for new human parents to supply their babies with clean diapers. After careful analysis of the mud compositions favored by mason bees, Crown Bees has determined a few things their preferred muds always have in common:

- no gravel
- no beauty bark
- no humus (decaying leaf or animal matter)
- no sand

All the particles we have found in the bees' mud have been smaller than a grain of sand. To briefly touch on soil science, you need to have either silt or sticky clay, two common types of dirt that are more finely grained than sand. Your native soil may not fit the bill, however, because it is too sandy or because you've added a lot of rich humus to your garden. Most plants enjoy humus as much as bees do not; if your garden exists only in containers, your soil likely leans heavily in this direction. To find the right bee-friendly material, try asking friends with a small stream on their property if you can bring some of the adjacent soil home. It is tough to find the right soil in a bag at the garden supply store, but home gardeners on Gardenweb.com and Reddit forums suggest contacting a company near you that installs in-ground swimming pools; their excavators dig deep enough to hit clay in many parts of the country. Crown Bees also sells a bee-approved, just-add-water mud mix.

If you are a casual gardener who doesn't care about a perfect green lawn, or you are a vegetable gardener who doesn't only rely on raised beds, it is entirely possible you have a little patch of suitable mud already, or at least a site where it would not trouble you to keep a mud patch accessible to your bees. It does not need to be prominent or easy for the human eye to spot—mason bees are well adapted to finding the mud they need. This means, of course, that if they do not find the mud they need in your yard, they will move on to a place where it—and other bee-friendly garden components—is available.

Along with being finely grained, the mud needs to stay in the damp-to-wet range: not soupy, but soft enough for a bee to pick it up in her tiny mandibles and pack it into her nest. A small, shovel-sized hole in the ground is the easiest solution, dug 10–20 feet (3–6 meters) away from the nesting tubes. At a minimum, aim for a hole that is 9 inches (23 centimeters) deep and about 9 inches square, although broader and deeper is completely fine. It's best to place your imported mud thickly on a shady wall of the hole.

Whether you need to place transplanted mud in the hole, or the mud in your garden is already the right texture, make sure to keep the moisture level as stable as you can. In climates with cool, fairly damp springs, nature typically takes care of this for you, but heavy morning dew can make bare ground too damp at times. In the afternoon the soil can dry out too much, forcing the bees to search elsewhere for collectible mud. If you live in an area with low humidity or springtime droughts, keep an eye on it and water as needed so it maintains an acceptable level of sticky moisture. If your mud dries out within a day, you can also purchase a mud box that uses capillary action to keep the mud moist for long periods.

Even if you think a patch of bare ground will suit your bees, it's a good idea to try digging a hole. With a hole in the ground, the bees will remember the right spot to collect their mud—like humans remember our favorite hardware stores—and you can more easily control the moisture level. Mason bees tend to mine the mud from a vertical surface, not a horizontal one. In the morning, they will collect their mud higher up in the hole (where it is less damp early in the day), and in the afternoon the mud collection activity will move down lower in the hole (where moisture has lingered).

Depending on where you live, frogs may find your bees' mud hole enchanting. In a mason bee–rearing enclosure near Bakersfield, California, Dr. Gordon Wardell once found a surprising number of unusually large, satiated-looking toads sitting in the enclosure's perfect mud pits. Needless to say, the researchers found a new home for these amphibians who had happened upon an all-you-can-eat mason bee buffet.

Your bees will thank you for your mud-related efforts by sticking around and doing their great pollination work right where you want them.

BRANCH OUT FOR LEAF BEES

Whereas mason bees require mud for their nesting material, leaf bees build with leaves. Like mason bees and their mud, leaf bees are fairly particular. They need specific types of leaves located within 100–200 feet (30–61 meters) of their nesting holes. Happily, the leaves they most prefer are found mainly on perennial plants, so unlike the mud for mason bees, there are no real demands on you as a gardener, once you've added a few of the right plants to your garden space. For those with yard space, a lilac or redbud tree, or a few rose bushes, will be enough to support many generations of leaf bees.

If your garden space is only in a community garden, or containers on an apartment balcony or rooftop space, trees or shrubs are likely not possible. Planting any kind of bean (either bush

Evidence of leaf bees at work—and harmless for the plant (Dave Hunter/Crown Bees)

type or pole type) or pea (snow, snap, shelling, or sweet peas) will do double duty as a compact crop for your kitchen and an excellent source of leaves for your leaf bees. Whichever plants you choose, don't spray them with any pesticides, and ask your neighbors to refrain as well if it's a shared gardening space.

HOME IS WHERE THE BEES ARE

When mason and leaf bees were intentionally added to the yards of a few forward-thinking organic gardeners in the late 1970s, it was commonly advised that you could simply take a block of wood—like a short chunk of 4-by-4 (10 centimeters by 10 centimeters)—and drill rows of ¼-to-⅜-inch (6-to-10-millimeter) holes in it, each a little larger than the diameter of a pencil. Attach that block of wood to a wall or post near your garden and you were good to go! Similar nesting blocks remain fairly common, and that's a shame for several reasons.

This style of home is as confusing to solitary bees as it would be for you to live in an apartment building where every single door was exactly the same color and did not have a prominent unit number on it. The bees can find their way back to the wood block, but they cannot easily tell their front door from their neighbors'. While it is possible to slightly improve on this simple design with a bit of exterior decoration so the entrance to each hole is visually different,

Drilled holes in a solid piece of wood are problematic homes for mason bees. (Dmitri Zelenevski/iStock)

NESTING TUBES: A COMPARISON

Mason bees are a bit larger than leaf bees, and their preferred nesting-cavity size coincides with the size of the adult bee. While the materials you can use are the same for both bees, the diameter should be different according to the type of bee you are housing. Whichever style you choose, know that your bees will have a preference for nesting holes with a securely sealed back.

PREFERRED NESTING HOLE SIZES

BEE	HOLE DIAMETER	HOLE DIAMETER APPROX. RANGE
MASON BEE	¼ to ¼" (6–9 mm)	
LEAF BEE	⅛ to ¼" (5–7 mm)	

PAPER

Pros: Inexpensive; easy to acquire

Cons: Needs to be rolled by hand or around pencils to create tubes of four overlapping layers, which can be tedious; new tubes are needed each year; can be fragile in wet and windy climates

Bee perspective: Fine if clean, arranged haphazardly and in assorted colors in the bee house, not perfect symmetry and evenness

CARDBOARD WITH INNER LINERS

Pros: Inexpensive; easy to harvest; layered construction reduces wasp access

Cons: Liners need to be replaced each year

Bee perspective: Fine if the tubes are clean and arranged haphazardly in the bee house

BAMBOO

Pros: Durable

Cons: Not recommended. Very difficult to open; typically too big a hole for mason bee use; unpredictable quality; prone to mold in damp climates

Bee perspective: Fine if they are sized correctly; each stalk of bamboo has a unique appearance, like reeds

NATURAL REED

Pros: Durable in challenging climates; convenient to order

Cons: A step up in price from paper or cardboard; easiest to open via a specially purchased reed splitter

Bee perspective: A fantastic place to start a family; preferred by most mason bees if correctly sized

WOODEN TRAY

Pros: Durable, easy to clean

Cons: More expensive up front; require a boxy frame or bands to hold them tightly together

Bee perspective: Least appeal; as long as they are clean and the exterior face has been patterned with paint or a torch to create a unique environment

DRILLED BLOCK OF WOOD

Pros: Easy to create

Cons: Not recommended. Can be overrun with pests after a few seasons because these cannot be opened up for cleaning

Bee perspective: Fine if new and clean; horrible after a season due to debris inside and pests waiting to eat pollen and eggs

BeeTubes and inserts with a back (left) or reeds (right) help prevent parasitic wasps from getting through the side walls to the valuable bee larvae. (Dave Hunter/Crown Bees)

it still has a fundamental problem: As a bee fills her home with eggs tucked into their little mud- or leaf-lined nests, mold spores, parasites, and pollen mites will also get inside. Sometimes after a single season, the invading pests make the wood block uninhabitable for bees, and they will die off or move elsewhere. Cleaning the holes in the blocks over the winter is impossible; you can lose an entire generation of bee cocoons in the process. Ultimately, these blocks are neither easy to care for nor sustainable.

To avoid these problems, the bees' nesting holes need to be either cleanable or disposable, each and every year. A clean and inexpensive alternative to old-fashioned blocks is a series of simple tubes that are open on one end, which can be crafted from a variety of natural materials. Hollow natural reeds are an excellent option because their unique sizes and shapes make them easy for bees to find. There are also premade paper tubes as well as a DIY paper version that can be made by wrapping folded paper around a pencil four times and securing it with a small piece of tape. Do not be tempted by plastic drinking straws: Plastic prevents excess moisture from wicking away from the cocoons, which can cause mold, and the holes are typically too small. Old-fashioned paper drinking straws, while an acceptable choice, are a little on the small side to be ideal—look for those with a wider diameter, sometimes labeled boba straws (but keep in mind that the paper walls will be thin enough to provide easy access for parasitic wasps). Although bamboo is hollow and can be found in the right diameter, it, unlike reeds, is typically too structurally solid to easily slice open without damaging the bee cocoons inside.

Leaf bees have similar requirements, though leaf bees are smaller than mason bees and thus use slightly smaller nesting holes—about ¼ inch (6 millimeters). Solitary beekeepers can use the same mason bee house to contain the tubes for leaf species, as the species pollinate in different

LEFT: *Through experimentation, the Crown Bees team found that bees prefer nesting holes that are unique versus monotonous in appearance.* (Dave Hunter/Crown Bees) RIGHT: *Optimal nesting materials: BeeTubes and inserts, reeds, and wood trays, which can all be safely opened up for fall mason bee harvest.* (Dave Hunter/Crown Bees)

seasons—simply exchange the larger mason bee tubes for smaller ones when the season is right.

An effective, more permanent alternative to these disposable tubes is layered racks of bee-friendly wooden trays; cut the exterior surface unevenly and scorch patchy patterns with a blowtorch (or a Dremel wood-burning accessory) to create easily identifiable entrances. These trays cost more up front but do not need to be replaced every year. Perhaps most importantly, they are extremely easy to separate at the end of a season, so you can remove cocoons for winter safekeeping and clean out any pests and their residue. The trays stack neatly in a square or rectangular shape and are available with precut 5⁄16-inch (8-millimeter) or ¼-inch (6-millimeter) holes. Ensure you use a backing on the rear of the trays. A dense filter between the cardboard backing and the wood tray prevents parasitic wasps from accessing the cocoons at the back of the nesting holes.

It may take some thought to determine which style suits you and the ongoing health of your bees the most, but several options are generally available through garden centers, nurseries, some hardware stores with good plant selections, or even a grocery store with a focus on organic products, from Whole Foods Market to your local food co-op (see Resources for online options).

These tubes or trays are gathered into a group and placed in a heavy-duty plastic or wooden container: Picture a birdhouse with no front panel. Instead of aligning the tubes into a uniformly flat surface, arrange them so some stick out while others are fully recessed to give the bees a clue as to which front door is theirs. Tucking a few twigs or other small natural objects between some of the tubes is another great way to help the bees find their way back home. While the house walls and roof can be painted, oiled, or varnished, complete these treatments at least 30 days in advance and place the parts in the sun before placing the houses outdoors for use—bees do not care for the smell of the paints. It is also fine to leave the wood unfinished.

Whatever shape you choose to contain your tubes or trays, you will notice something fun as your bees make themselves at home. Like people moving into new apartment buildings, they have preferences when it comes to where in the building they live. Bees tend to first choose the holes on the corners and the bottom floor, then they will move toward the center, and the penthouse spots are the last to go. In the case of bees, it's unlikely it is the neighbor's noise or the steeper rent for the units on the top floor, but simply that the holes they choose first are the easiest to find.

Try not to leave much empty space between the top row of nesting holes and the roof of the house, since those spaces make great bird-nesting locations or wasp homes. Fill this vacant space with sticks or paper—or another, more attractive, material, as long as it fills the space.

LOCATION, LOCATION, LOCATION

Once you have selected and combined your nesting tubes and frame, it is time to hang it up. Choosing the correct corner of your house or side of your garage can make all the difference to the health and comfort of your bees. Here are factors to consider:

- For your own enjoyment, choose a spot near your eye level (or the eye level of any junior scientists you might have at home). The bees will not mind you watching them at work or walking past them.
- If your region is prone to summer storms, make sure the box has adequate shelter from wind, hail, or heavy downpours.

A mud box can be easily used in yards without moist clay. (Dave Hunter/Crown Bees)

- When it comes to sunshine, the best combination is plenty of morning sun with shade that kicks in during the hottest part of the day, usually midafternoon. Not enough sun, and the bees will start each day sluggishly; too much, and their eggs will be cooked to a crisp on hot summer days. Afternoon heat is a bigger concern in places where spring temperatures can be decidedly hot rather than merely warm. In cool, overcast regions, mason bees will appreciate the warmth of daylong full sun.
- For mason bees, ensure there is a source of moist, clayey mud within 20 feet (6 meters), while for leaf bees, have plenty of their preferred leaves within 20 feet (6 meters).
- While leaf bees are warm-weather bees, it's still best for their houses to not get many hours of direct sun. Again, it's fine in the coolest part of the day, but they should be given shade when afternoon temperatures are at their peak.

TOP 10 NATIVE PLANTS FOR POLLINATORS IN SEVEN REGIONS

The following list of native plants that attract pollinators, including mason bees, comes courtesy of the National Garden Club (gardenclub.org), with supplementation from USDA regional guides, and is a helpful starting point for choosing native plants that range from wildflowers and ground covers to vines, shrubs, and trees. Almost every US state and Canadian province has a native plant society. You can locate yours thanks to the North American Native Plant Society (nanps.org), which can direct you to local resources and information. With their help, you can fine-tune this list to suit your garden's microclimate as well as your own style preferences. Plants with leaves appealing to a variety of leaf bees are marked with an icon.

NORTHEAST US (MAINE TO NEW YORK), SOUTHERN QUEBEC, SOUTHEASTERN ONTARIO

» American witchhazel (*Hamamelis virginiana*)
» bigleaf aster (*Eurybia macrophylla*)
» black-eyed Susan (*Rudbeckia hirta*)
» hookedspur violet (*Viola adunca*)
» kinnikinnick (*Arctostaphylos uva-ursi*)
» northern bush honeysuckle (*Diervilla lonicera*)
» roundleaf dogwood (*Cornus rugosa*)
» swamp milkweed (*Asclepias incarnata*)
» trailing arbutus (*Epigaea repens*)
» white meadowsweet (*Spiraea alba*)

SOUTHEAST US (MARYLAND TO GEORGIA, WEST TO MISSISSIPPI AND EAST TEXAS)

» coral honeysuckle (*Lonicera sempervirens*)
» eastern redbud (*Cercis canadensis*)
» Georgia savory (*Clinopodium georgianum*)
» green hawthorn (*Crataegus viridis*)
» hairy sunflower (*Helianthus hirsutus*)
» Maryland golden-aster (*Chrysopsis mariana*)
» oakleaf hydrangea (*Hydrangea quercifolia*)
» pawpaw (*Asimina triloba*)
» swamp rose (*Rosa palustris*)
» Walter's violet (*Viola walteri*)

LEFT: *Black-eyed Susans* (Bryan Reynolds) RIGHT: *Coral honeysuckle* (Bryan Reynolds)

MIDWEST US (NORTH DAKOTA TO MISSOURI, EAST TO INDIANA), SOUTHERN MANITOBA, SOUTHWESTERN ONTARIO

- beebalm (*Monarda* sp.)
- black-eyed Susan (*Rudbeckia hirta*)
- chokecherry (*Prunus virginiana*)
- longbract wild indigo (*Baptisia bracteata*)
- milkweed: prairie and swamp species (*Asclepias sullivantii, A. incarnata*)
- New Jersey tea (*Ceanothus americanus*)
- phlox (*Phlox* sp.)
- prairie clover (*Dalea* sp.)
- sumac (*Rhus* sp.)
- willow (*Salix* sp.)

ROCKIES (MONTANA AND IDAHO TO NEW MEXICO), SOUTHERN SASKATCHEWAN, ALBERTA

- American vetch (*Vicia americana*)
- Colorado blue columbine (*Aquilegia coerulea*)
- creeping barberry (*Mahonia repens*)
- fivepetal cliffbush (*Jamesia americana*)
- hairy false goldenaster (*Heterotheca villosa*)
- Lewis flax (*Linum lewisii*)
- pony beebalm (*Monarda pectinata*)
- Porter's licorice root (*Ligusticum porteri*)
- prairie bluebell (*Mertensia lanceolata*)
- wholeleaf Indian paintbrush (*Castilleja integra*)

SOUTHWEST US (NEVADA, UTAH, ARIZONA, SOUTHERN CALIFORNIA)

- Bigelow's nolina (*Nolina bigelovii*)
- cactus apple (*Cereus repandus*)
- common sotol (*Dasylirion wheeleri*)
- Mojave lupine (*Lupinus sparsiflorus*)
- ocotillo (*Fouquieria splendens*)
- Parry's beardtongue (*Penstemon parryi*)
- teddybear cholla (*Cylindropuntia bigelovii*)

(continued on next page)

TOP TO BOTTOM: *Downy phlox* (Bryan Reynolds); *American vetch* (Larry Eiden/Shutterstock); *Velvet mesquite* (Pritha_EasyArts/Shutterstock)

- velvet mesquite (*Prosopis velutina*)
- white tepary bean (*Phaseolus acutifolius*)
- yellow paloverde (*Parkinsonia microphylla*)

CALIFORNIA CENTRAL VALLEY

- California buckeye (*Aesculus californica*)
- California poppy (*Eschscholzia californica*)
- California redbud (*Cercis occidentalis*)
- milkweed: woollypod, California, and narrow-leaved species (*Asclepias eriocarpa, A. californica, A. fascicularis*)
- summer lupine (*Lupinus formosus*)
- telegraph weed (*Heterotheca grandiflora*)
- thistle sage (*Salvia carduacea*)
- toyon (*Heteromeles arbutifolia*)
- yarrow (*Achillea millefolium*)
- yellow mariposa (*Calochortus luteus*)

PACIFIC NORTHWEST US (WASHINGTON, OREGON, NORTHERN CALIFORNIA) SOUTHERN BRITISH COLUMBIA

- bigleaf maple (*Acer macrophyllum*)
- California hazelnut (*Corylus cornuta* var. *californica*)
- Oregon grape (*Mahonia aquifolium*)
- redwood violet (*Viola sempervirens*)
- salal (*Gaultheria shallon*)
- trailing blackberry (*Rubus ursinus*)
- trillium (*Trillium* sp.)
- vine maple (*Acer circinatum*)
- western buttercup (*Ranunculus occidentalis*)
- woodland strawberry (*Fragaria vesca*)

TOP TO BOTTOM: *California poppy* (Tamara Kulikova/ Shutterstock); *Oregon grape* (Svetlana Mahovskaya/ Shutterstock); *Salal* (Steve Estvanik/Shutterstock)

- If mounting the house on a post in an orchard or garden space, think ahead about where trees or walls provide shade. If you are raising mason bees, remember that the foliage that arrives along with or shortly after blossom time may create shade on the entrance when you intend it to have full sun. Think ahead to a spot that will not be in a shadow when the trees are fully leafed out or be difficult to access as the year's new branches have lengthened.
- If you have a bird feeder, the best solution is to move it elsewhere during mason bee season, keeping the two structures out of each other's line of sight. If birds are prevalent, refer to pages 55–56 for protection advice.

PLANTS AND POLLEN

With their necessary mud or leaves and a nicely located home, mason and leaf bees are ready to get to work. But not all gardens are created equal, because these days, not all plants are created equal.

Imagine two lush, flowering container plants side by side on a patio. Both are abundantly colorful, and both offer plenty of cheery yellow and blue blooms, colors that bees love every bit as much as hummingbirds are said to adore red. Color will be the only thing both planters have in common, since it is a casual piece of information that many garden center employees latch on to when they help you shop for plants.

But that is where the similarity ends. Container number one was grown from organic seed that was never chemically treated; it took a bit of patience to establish, but from spring through midsummer it is fragrant with sweet alyssum and flowering lemon thyme. It has taller cornflower and chamomile in the center, and cheerful four o'clocks are mixed in for late-afternoon appeal. Barring a vicious winter, many of these plants will happily reseed themselves or, in the case of thyme, grow as an evergreen perennial. You can even brew the tiny yellow and white chamomile flowers into a cup of iced tea to enjoy on the porch.

Container number two was quickly created from inexpensive, sterile hybrid, "basket-stuffer" plants common at large home-and-garden chains. The plants were chemically treated

BE HOA-AWARE

If your residence falls within the governance of a homeowners association (HOA), read through their guidelines concerning landscaping before tearing up your existing garden. Some home gardeners have made national headlines or found themselves the subject of a lawsuit when simply adding edible garden containers to their front yards. Some HOAs allow a broader range of planting but pay for commercial pesticide-spraying services. Sometimes, you can plant whatever you like within a fenced backyard but must conform to specific rules for whatever's in front of the house. The best thing you may be able to do for pollinators is to join your HOA and get those rules adjusted to accommodate native plants or to discontinue commercial-spraying contracts. Each HOA is different in what it allows, and informing yourself is the smartest first step.

POLLINATOR PLANTS FOR PATIOS

Small-scale flowering herbs are a terrific choice for attracting an array of wild pollinators to your balcony containers or rooftop gardens, and starting them from organic seed helps you avoid possible nursery-plant pesticide treatments that may be bee unfriendly. (See Resources for recommended seed companies.)

TISANE CONTAINER

- anise hyssop
- chamomile
- common or culinary sage
- licorice

HERBAL MEDICINE CONTAINER

- clary sage
- feverfew
- holy basil
- licorice

EDIBLE FLOWER CONTAINER

- agastache
- borage
- nasturtium
- calendula

Phacaelia, a sweet-smelling member of the borage family, is attractive to many pollinators, and makes a long-lasting cut flower. (Jill Lightner)

before their arrival at the store so they would be resistant to disease and pests up through their point of purchase (as well as into the period after you have planted them). The mix of double-blossom fuchsias, yellow jessamine, lobelia, and morning glories looks pretty and even smells good, thanks to the powerful fragrance of the jessamine.

Unfortunately, the second planter is only enjoyable for humans. Double-blossomed fuchsias are difficult to pollinate. Fragrant jessamine can be toxic to bees. Heavily hybridized modern lobelia and morning glory varieties offer little to no pollen. How distressing to think that plants that add beauty to your porch or patio can do harm!

This is not to say that all plants you grow must be selected with only bees in mind—that is as limiting as saying you will live on kale forever and never again touch a dessert. Remember to think of bees as dedicated partners in your garden ecosystem, and plant some things they will enjoy as much as you will love your ruffled hybrid flowers.

Some perennials, such as lavender, are known for their happy ability to attract bees by the dozen. When they are in full bloom, the whole plant will be abuzz from midmorning through the early evening with a busy, and attractive, collection of solitary and social bees. There are also well-known herbs such as beebalm, whose name makes its compatibility apparent, and popular culinary herbs such as anise hyssop and borage do an excellent job of attracting a variety of bees. Also look for the less common bees' friend (*Bienenfreund* in German, and more officially *Phacelia tanacetifolia*), with delicate, lacy periwinkle flowers and a sweet fragrance.

Instead of focusing on any particular plant, remember that not all flowers are accessible to all bees, and not all flowers benefit equally from the same type of bee. While mason bees are active when blueberries are in flower, the flowers tend to be too small for mason bees to gather pollen from them; those are best pollinated by bumble bees, which use a "buzz pollination" technique, going underneath each flower and causing the pollen to cascade down on top of their furry bodies. The fluffy, nub-shaped blooms of California lilac suit the bumble bees' technique as well as the crawling style of mason and leaf bees. Providing a variety of plants attracts a variety of pollinators, which will in turn benefit the broadest possible scope of plants—and a nice variety is possible even when your garden space is nothing more than a row of decent-sized pots on your apartment balcony.

If you currently have a lawn, you could work with a local native-plant landscaper, using regenerative techniques to remove what grass you have and replace it with a mix of ground covers and shrubs that flower at slightly different times. Many kinds of thyme are dense and walkable, with small attractive flowers that bees adore. The visual effect is of a low-growing meadow of tiny blooms; you can mix and match

IN PRAISE OF CLOVER

If you are willing to let one of the many varieties of clover take over a patch of ground, you might be surprised by its incredibly sweet fragrance and the absolute love many species of pollinators have for it. As a little underground bonus, clover feeds nitrogen back into garden soil, which many plants will find highly beneficial. Depending on your climate and the variety, it will bloom anytime from late spring through the end of summer. Most species are edible—by humans, deer, and livestock—and some spread more rapidly than others (see Resources for online seed companies).

JOE DLUGO

WILDLIFE GARDENER

Joe Dlugo has been a gardener for most of his life, first near Chicago and now—with multiple acres for the first time—in western Washington. His interest in attracting wildlife began with a specific bird, the ruby-throated hummingbird, which was then a rarity in that part of Illinois. Dlugo said, "I planted a garden with tubular, hummingbird-oriented flowers like salvia, and native plants that hummingbirds enjoyed, like beebalm and cardinal flower. It took several months, but a few hummers eventually showed up! I was hooked."

Today, his garden demonstrates how the right kind of human effort can result in a wildlife paradise. "After 12 years of living here, there is hardly a square meter that isn't accounted for in regard to wildlife value. I have gardens with plentiful native plants, shrublands, floodplain deciduous forest, and Douglas-firs." He treats moles as a partner, not a nuisance: "Their presence is so welcome, as they aerate the hard-packed Tenino soil. What they kick up in their mounds is usually great earth for adding to the garden. So, harvest that mole mound soil!"

Dlugo's experience may not work for those with less space or a strict HOA, but his perspective inspires. An imperfect lawn may be a perfect habitat. "For ground-nesting bees, I provide a lawn that very odd societal norms would characterize as beat up, but is truly a celebration of life. I have an area where there was an old swing set and kids trampled for years, with the soil compaction left behind being an extraordinary place for [those] bees," said Dlugo.

His acres are home to many wild pollinator species that he enjoys photographing and identifying. He aims to capture how bees genuinely look, which isn't always how artists portray them. At your next opportunity, take the time to notice what Dlugo has: "Many of our bees are green, not yellow and black stripes. It's just so unexpected, and so beautiful." Interested in learning to identify your region's wild bee species? As an admirer of the Washington Native Bee Society, Dlugo suggests finding a similar group in your area, as there's no identification app or book quite as useful as an in-person expert.

On the matter of plant selection, Dlugo appreciates how the right blend of native and nonnative plants work together to keep pollinators thriving. He notes that the native plants are what draw less common species to his garden, but in western Washington, most have short blooming seasons. "That's when you can strategically mix in the ornamental varieties and their typically longer bloom times to keep the bees going." He specifically praises an easy-to-grow herb that does well across much of the continent. "For loads of bees, a very long bloom, and almost no maintenance, you can't go wrong with planting *Nepeta* (catmint). It's not native, but it's awesome, especially when it comes to small, cavity-nesting native bees such as *Osmia* sp. (mason bees) and bumble bees." Gardening websites like to note that catmint "thrives on neglect," making it a clear winner for those who prefer to laze in the garden.

flower color and leaf texture as you see fit. Once established, thymes need less water than grass to stay green and appealing, they never need mowing, and their spicy, herbaceous fragrance when stepped on is an added bonus. This is a yard that will be the envy of neighbors walking by! The hard work here ends once the grass is removed.

Adding an early-blooming fruit tree to your yard is another potentially low-maintenance way of extending the months when you will have pollen-laden flowers easily available for bees. If you are not interested in harvesting anything yourself, trees of the genus *Amelanchier* (called serviceberry, among other names) grow in different varieties across North America, tending to flower early, and birds will nibble on their small, tart fruits later in the fall. Sweet or sour cherries are another good choice for early blossoms, followed in later spring by other stone fruits, apples, pears, citrus, and persimmons. If you are new to the realm of fruit trees, chat with a nursery expert or Master Gardener in your area before choosing one, as many regions have specific pests or diseases that make some fruits very high maintenance or impossible to grow organically. If you are adding a tree in part for your bees, you do not want to select one that requires a chemical spray right when it is

Ideal leaves for bees, such as rose and lilac, are easily cut and carried. (SusanneSchultz/iStock)

blossoming, as that would end up doing your pollinator crew more harm than good and can be lethal to eggs and subsequent larvae.

If you have introduced leaf bees along with (or instead of) mason bees, they will find a midsummer vegetable patch (beans, squash, and tomatoes are all good choices) or later-season fruits such as lingonberries, blueberries, blackberries, or marionberries appealing, as these bees thrive best when daytime temperatures are at least in the 80s Fahrenheit (high 20s Celsius). In general, it is easy to find plants that flower in midsummer, so if a bumper crop of beans is not what you want in your garden, make sure that you have a nice mix of pollen-filled flowers and the leaf bees will be happy. Planting flowers in clumps of 3 feet by 3 feet (1 meter by 1 meter) puts more pollen resources in one place, which is more effective than inefficiently spreading them across the yard. Bees prefer such clusters over individual flowers.

CHAPTER 3

MASON BEES: WHAT TO DO WHEN

Now that you have a sense of what your bees will need to thrive, you need to learn what is expected in terms of maintenance throughout the year. The short answer: It takes only a couple of hours of effort each year to keep mason bees. The long answer revolves around the knowledge and commitment needed for a few small tasks in each season of the year. Remember that the pollinating, flying part of a mason bee's life is only four to six weeks; they spend more than 10 months tucked into their cocoons.

WINTER: PLANNING AND INVENTORY

The heart of winter—around the time that gloriously colorful seed catalogs arrive—is the perfect time to prepare for setting your bees outside once it warms up. As you would when you look through those catalogs, all you need to do is curl up with a warm drink and do some planning.

If this is the first spring you will be adding bees to your garden, you need to consider the location of your mason bee house. If this is not your first year, evaluate whether last year's bee house was in the best possible spot.

HOW MANY MASON BEES FOR MY SPACE?

- 20 mason bee cocoons for a 200-square-foot (18.5-square-meter) patio with two fruit trees and flower containers
- 30 mason bee cocoons for a 2,500-square-foot (232-square-meter) yard with three fruit trees and flower beds
- 100 mason bee cocoons for a ¼-acre (0.1-hectare) yard with eight fruit trees and flower beds
- 400 mason bee cocoons for a 1-acre (0.4-hectare) community orchard
- 1,000 mason bee cocoons for a 1-acre (0.4-hectare) commercial cherry orchard (more densely planted than a typical community garden)
- Want to bring mason bees to New York's Central Park? You would need about 300,000 mason bee cocoons to cover its 843 acres (341 hectares)!

Remember that morning sun wakes your bees up early, leading to more time spent pollinating. Pause and recall whether you planted any new trees last fall, or consider whether a neighbor's recent landscaping or remodeling project might have affected last year's prime spot. For those in hot climates, if you cut down or pruned back plants that created afternoon shade for your bees, you may need to relocate your bee house.

Next, determine how many cocoons you need, which involves a little guesswork if this is your first year. In a commercial orchard you would want around 1,000 cocoons for 100 trees. This ratio applies to the sort of orchard where all 100 trees are in bloom at nearly the same time. Ten cocoons per blooming tree will ensure that plenty of pollination work can happen all at once.

A home garden is less likely to have everything burst into bloom the same week, so these numbers should be scaled down. Typically, you'll want 20 cocoons to begin with, at a minimum, even for a small, urban container garden. A moderate number, in the realm of 100, is suitable for a small community garden.

Because one mason bee can potentially create up to 20 cocoons each year, every year that you keep mason bees, the number of bees should grow naturally for the next year. This year's bees are laying next year's bees. As a loose, bare minimum, you should be able to double your bee population each year. This is not only impressive all by itself but also amazing when you consider how quickly you can dramatically boost the number of pollinators in your neighborhood. As your bee population grows, you need to make sure you have the right number of nesting holes; this is the second step in your annual inventory process. If you are starting with 20 cocoons, you will need about 20 to 30 straws, tubes, or holes (as described in chapter 2), or about one hole per cocoon.

If you are new to mason bees, you can order your bee cocoons online to be shipped to you at the right time for setting outside in your specific environment, much like when you order flower bulbs or a nursery plant.

If you have been managing your own cocoon inventory each fall and storing them over the winter, it will not be long before you need to share cocoons with another interested gardener, which is part of the fun of keeping mason bees. They are a bit like maintaining a sourdough starter or managing a zucchini harvest: At first you worry about having enough for your own needs, then you have exactly the correct amount, and suddenly you start looking around in desperation, searching for a home where your extras will be appreciated.

As you share excess cocoons, make sure to advise your neighbor on how to choose their own ideal bee house location, while making sure their bees' nesting holes are of a good material. After a single season of keeping mason bees, you will be looked to as a local expert! It is also a great time for a friendly conversation if you suspect your neighbor might be using some garden chemicals that are not bee friendly. Even if your immediate neighbors are not interested, it is still generally easy to find a home for extra cocoons. If you have coworkers who garden, see if they are interested, or check with a nearby community garden. Check in with your local garden clubs or a nearby "Buy Nothing" group (look for group pages on social media; sometimes a single city will have multiple groups). You can even offer them for free through Craigslist or similar forums (or sign up for Crown Bees' Bee Buy Back program, page 68). If your church has a garden, ask a staff member whether they would like a gift of gentle bees. We think it is more fun to find as direct a connection as possible: Aside from providing an opportunity for a little bee-vangelism on healthy gardening practices, building a sense of community among mason beekeepers helps increase their popularity. And

Protect mason bees from hungry birds with a bird guard. (Dave Hunter/Crown Bees)

more well-kept bees and an increased population of pollinators benefit us all.

Birds and Bees

Winter is also the right time to get ahead of any "bird buffet" problems your bee house experienced in the past—birds are a common issue, particularly if you have a backyard bird feeder, but it is one that is easy to solve. A quick, effective correction: Make sure that your bee house and your bird feeder are not too close to each other. In general, birds are not as picky about their location as mason bees, so it is best to choose the spot for your bee house first and then move the birdhouse or feeder as necessary.

Woodpeckers can be problematic. Considering that they evolved to pluck insects and larvae from narrow holes in wood, they are only doing their job by removing bee cocoons from your bee house. Remind yourself that wild mason bees have likely moved into the holes that these same woodpeckers created in trees; these birds and insects have a close, natural relationship in many different ecosystems. Still, to protect your own mason bees, cover the front of the bee house with ¾-inch (2-centimeter) galvanized wire mesh, available at most hardware stores. Crown Bees also offers Bird Guard galvanized screens, premeasured to specific styles and sizes of bee houses. Wire-mesh squares of this size don't impact bee access but make the bee house much more difficult for jays and woodpeckers to access. When you install the panel, create a 2-inch (5-centimeter) bubble around the front of the house. Do not install the wire flush against the nesting materials as this can also prevent bees from accessing the nests.

Sometimes, the box that holds the bee nesting tubes has extra room at the top, creating an inviting spot for small birds to build their nests. You can prevent unwanted nests by filling the space with rocks or sticks or covering it with additional galvanized wire mesh.

TABLE 3.1. MASON BEE CARE TIMELINE

DAYTIME TEMPERATURE	WHAT TO DO
50–55°F (10–13°C), week 1	Release ⅓ of the cocoons.*
50–55°F, week 3	Release ⅓ of the cocoons.*
50–55°F, week 5	Release ⅓ of the cocoons.*
80°F (27°C), week 10 (This should be about 5 weeks after final release, or when no activity is seen.)	Collect all mason bee nesting tubes. Keep them outside (or in a shed) in a protective mesh bag, out of direct sunlight.
First day of fall	Harvest cocoons from nesting tubes and store for winter in a HumidiBee or similar container.
Mid-November	Check the moisture level and for the presence of mold in the cocoon storage container; add water or rinse off as needed.
Mid-December	Check the moisture level and for the presence of mold; add water or rinse off as needed.
Mid-January	Check the moisture level and for the presence of mold; add water or rinse off as needed.
Mid-February	Check the moisture level and for the presence of mold; add water or rinse off as needed.

*Note: About ⅔ of them should be females each time.

Mason Bees and Climate Change

Wherever you live, you are likely experiencing changes to formerly reliable weather patterns, easily spotted in whatever new climate records are being set. In the Pacific Northwest we have seen fresh records set for the highest rainfall in a single day as well as the most days without rain, in addition to both the hottest day and the out-of-season coldest day—all of these since 2018. Many new records are being set in every region.

Needless to say, nobody knows for sure what the next decade will offer us. So, instead of choosing a specific date to set out your bees, you will need to go by your plants' behavior and your local temperature *this* year, not last year, to set your bees out at the right time for them to find the best food supply (see Table 3.1). When mason bees have the pollen and nectar they need to thrive, their pollination efforts play a key role in ensuring that humans have a good food supply in later months.

Mason bee cocoons ready to place out (M Huston/ Shutterstock)

SPRING: MASON BEE EMERGENCE AND POLLINATION

Every region has its own first signs of spring, and the length of the season varies from one region to the next. In the typically cool and damp Pacific Northwest, spring can kick off in February, where we might see a week of daytime temperatures in the low 70s Fahrenheit (low 20s Celsius). All too frequently, things settle back down to the 40s (single digits Celsius) for several weeks after that. New England, on the other hand, can see winter snow last into early April, while the Front Range of the Rockies might get a blizzard in May. It is important not to rush things.

In most cases around the continent, shoots from a few early bulbs are considered the first sign of spring. But retrain your brain in this regard: The earliest bulb blossoms are more like a sign that winter is ending than spring is truly beginning. Kurt Vonnegut (a man known more for his novels than for his gardening) once suggested that we add a season between winter and spring called "unlocking," and that is a great way of looking at it: Enjoy the first show of earliest blossoms, but know that it is still a little too chilly for mason bees.

Instead, look for signs that the earliest fruit trees are ready to bloom. These might be plum, sweet cherry, or serviceberry. When these trees are breaking into blossom, the time is right for setting out a portion of your hibernating mason bees, perhaps one-third of them. As the first blossoms become more prevalent, and later-blooming varieties such as apple, peach, sour cherry, crab apple, and pear start flowering, set

As fruit trees blossom, it's time to put out your mason bee cocoons for the year. (Bryan Reynolds)

out your remaining bees. One-third of your bees every other week is a good approximate schedule to extend their pollinating time to the fullest. Have all your bees in place by no later than early May, as your fruit trees should be well in bloom by then. If you wait much longer, you risk causing the overwintered bees to run out of nutrients to live on inside their cocoons.

Sometimes a region can experience a seriously delayed spring, and this can create an issue for your bees. Mason bees survive winter by consuming their stored fats during hibernation. By keeping your cocoons in a refrigerator (see Fall: Cleaning and Storing Mason Bee Cocoons for the Future later in this chapter), you keep your bees' metabolism low and help their stored fat reserves last longer. Even with help from the cool stability of your fridge's temperature, though, the bees have evolved to emerge sooner than the first of May. If they are not buzzing around your yard by that date, you will find males emerging from their cocoons in your refrigerator, as they are hungry and have run out of their stored fat reserve. A small cotton ball soaked in a mixture of 50 percent granulated sugar and 50 percent water will provide them with calories for survival. (Do not substitute any other form of sweetener for the granulated sugar.) If you are waiting for outside temperatures to catch up with your bees' needs, keep the emerged males with their soaked cotton ball in a dark paper lunch sack within their refrigerator container.

Once your bees are using their nesting holes, do not move the house or individual nesting tubes. Mason bees will leave if their environment changes. If you are not satisfied with the location of your bee house, consider adding another one in a new location to see which the bees prefer instead of relocating the house in the middle of the bee's short lifespan.

Beginning mid-April, or three weeks after you have set out all your mason bees, count how many nesting holes have been filled up by nesting females. If a female finishes up a nest hole and cannot find another empty one to use, she will fly off in search of a fresh spot. It is easy to tuck in additional nesting holes (tubes, straws, or reeds) on top of existing holes or to add another wooden tray or two if you went with the stackable tray design. Remember, when adding more, do not disturb the original holes.

A Bee's Life: A Busy Six Weeks

The male bees are the first to emerge from their cocoons. Their lives are only about two weeks long from the moment they emerge, compared with six weeks for females. In species-survival terms, the role they have is a brief one, as they are only involved in reproduction. You will see them emerge, fly around to pollen sources for food, then hover around the straws or emergence box waiting for the females to break out of their cocoons.

Placing Out Cocoons

Mason bees will emerge quickly if the temperatures are in the low 50s Fahrenheit (10 degrees or more Celsius). Try placing the cocoons behind or on top of the nesting holes, if your bee hotel does not have a drawer designed as a cocoon hatchery. This way, the newly emerged bees will crawl over the holes and typically will memorize their new home and know how to find it again after flying off to find pollen. Watch out for direct, hot sun on the cocoons, as intense heat may kill them, and it is best to set them out on a

ATTRACTING WILD MASON BEES

Mason bees are native to all but the most humid areas of the United States, and it is possible to attract your own wild bees instead of purchasing your first set of cocoons or to simply provide a healthy home for wild bees. The combination of a pheromone spray (a scent attractant) on natural reeds (a visual attractant) is a good way of attracting wild mason bees. These sprays, such as Crown Bees' InvitaBee, are available online (see Resources) and at some garden nurseries. Spray the reeds and tuck them into your bee house (even if the rest of your nesting tubes are another material, a few reeds should be able to fit into your nesting hole design, although you may have to get creative about it).

Wild bees will vary in size more than purchased bees, and small bees use small nesting holes while larger ones need bigger tubes. If wild bees are your goal, provide a range of nesting tube diameters from $\frac{5}{32}$ inch (4 millimeters) to $\frac{3}{8}$ inch (10 millimeters). Some people suggest that painting parts of the bee house with patches of blue or yellow—the same colors they prefer in flowers—is another helpful way of attracting bees.

TOP: *Blue orchard mason bee cocoons: the smaller male (left), larger female (right)* (Dave Hunter/ Crown Bees) BOTTOM: *Early morning or evening are the best times to catch a mason bee resting near filled nesting tubes.* (Jill Lightner)

day when strong winds are not blowing through your neighborhood. Birds can be another threat: Before the bees emerge, the cocoons are a snack sitting in plain sight.

When setting out cocoons every other week, you want to make sure that you have a mix of males and females each time. It is fairly easy to spot the difference, as female cocoons are noticeably larger; on average, the males are about 30 percent smaller. As long as you select a broad mix of sizes when you place your cocoons outside, you should be in good shape.

After the males hatch, the females will follow, mate with the males, and begin scouting your yard for pollen, nesting holes, and mud of the right texture. If they find these essentials (described in detail in chapter 2), they should start nesting in your mason bee house. Nesting means they are making a few dozen trips around the flowers for the material to create a pea-size ball of nutritious pollen and nectar in the back of their chosen nesting hole. They will cement a single egg onto that pollen-nectar mass then make about 10 trips to the mud patch, gathering enough finely textured mud to seal the egg's chamber.

If you are having a dry spring, remember to keep your mud patch damp. The mud that mason bees need for their nests is so finely textured that it turns to dust quickly in low-humidity environments. While most regions can count on regular spring rain or moisture from snowmelt, that is not uniformly true across the continent, and even generally wet places can have a spring drought. Even if you do not need to water your plants yet, you may need to water the mud for your bees. Remember that damp mud, not soupy mud, is easiest for bees to pick up in their tiny mandibles. You may want to create a system

Peek inside the tubes to spot the bees' iridescent heads. (Jill Lightner)

to guarantee moist mud—by wicking water from a container underneath—for your bees. A capillary cloth dipped into stored water can keep your mud moist for weeks on end.

Once you have set out your first group of cocoons, it is easy to get a little anxious. Are they hatching? Did you miss anything critical? Did those mysterious little egg-shaped, paper-like cocoons truly have bees inside them? If it is warm enough (in the high 50s Fahrenheit or around 15 degrees Celsius), you might see males begin hatching after a few hours, but you will usually need some patience. With cool nighttime temperatures or a dip in the daytime temperature, it could be several days before you notice activity. A light brown, muddy-looking substance on the mason bee holes or house is a great sign of first activity: This is meconium, a metabolic waste that the bees poop out within minutes of emerging. Then you will notice several bees going in and out of the tubes or trays, although it is harder to spot them on your plants.

Once you notice your first completed tube, loaded with egg chambers and sealed off with a thick mud wall by a female bee, you will feel like celebrating. A filled mason bee nesting tube may look plain (it is only a tan tube sealed with mud!), but the thrill is about the same as the first time you spot a colorful songbird at a new feeder.

The Lessons of Failure

Sometimes things go awry, even when all conditions should translate into success. Perhaps few bees emerge, or they emerge but then disappear. Did a neighbor spray their garden? Were you misled at the garden center where you bought your supplies? Our problem-solving brains want clear solutions—and failing that, we want someone to blame. Mason bee companies hear many success stories, but sometimes things simply do not work out, and an obvious fix is not available. If you do not experience success, do not quietly give up. Try connecting with an expert

SEASONAL ALERT!

If you also keep leaf bees, the end of spring and beginning of summer is when your leaf bees should emerge. Refer to chapter 4 for the correct temperatures and schedule.

or successful mason beekeeper and see if they have some advice or guesses; a different perspective might do the trick. And do not think sharing your failure means you did something wrong or that mason bees are not "worth it." Something about your particular lack of success might lead the way to a whole new area of study for researchers or bring an issue to the forefront of discussion among your community's mason bee advocates.

Storing filled tubes in fine mesh fabric protects cocoons over the summer. (Dave Hunter/Crown Bees)

SUMMER: MASON BEE PROTECTION

Early to mid-June is typically the ideal time to remove mason bee nesting tubes from their outdoor home. Tending to this now will reduce the likelihood that the bee larvae will run into problems from Houdini flies or other common pests.

To store the tubes over the summer, gently remove them from their box, leaving them intact. Place them upright (with mud-sealed ends pointed upward) in a vented container somewhere like a garage, barn, or shed. This is not the time to store them in a cool basement or refrigerator, as the larvae inside the tubes are quietly forming their tough little cocoons and storing nutrients to sustain them through the winter. The ideal temperature is whatever the average outside temperature is where you live, minus the extra heat from direct sunlight. Store them well away from windows and uninsulated walls that get hours of unimpeded sun.

It is important to keep the nesting tubes protected from parasitic wasps or small rodents. Rather than tucking them completely out of sight, put them somewhere where you can keep a casual eye on them. For example, Crown Bees makes a bag called a BeeGuard, from industrial-strength organza with double drawstring closures. The ideal material is a strong, fine mesh

FRASS ID

Other than mud and cocoons, the one thing that you should expect to see when you clean cocoons is frass, or poop from the bee larva. Frass will cling slightly to the exterior of each cocoon; you may also find it on the tray or tubes or the walls between cocoons. These small, dark brown pellets are not a pest and nothing to be concerned about.

that allows good ventilation but prevents pests from getting in easily. A similar option is the 941.08 Wasp-Proof Storage Bag from Beediverse, made of finely woven mesh and closed with heavy drawstrings. If you are comfortable with a DIY craft project, you can stitch or glue heavy-duty organza into a similar nesting-tube protection bag. The size should accommodate your nesting tubes in a vertical position and shut securely enough that tiny predators cannot get in. Drawstrings are better than Velcro, as it is difficult to seal the ends of a Velcro strip, and ants and tiny wasps can crawl into the bag through almost invisible gaps. Pests can be persistent—the protection of a bag will pay off!

PEST PATROL

Concerned about what you're spotting near your bee house in the summer or with your cocoons in the fall? Look to the following sections to identify and manage mason bee pests:

- pollen mites, page 88
- chalkbrood fungus, page 89
- Houdini flies, page 90
- mono wasps, page 91
- Sapygidae (sapygid or club-horned) wasps, page 93
- moth and beetle larvae, page 94

FALL: CLEANING AND STORING MASON BEE COCOONS FOR THE FUTURE

September to mid-October is the time to harvest your mason bee cocoons. If you are tempted to skip this step, remember that you will be greatly increasing the likelihood that your bees will run into problems with any of several common parasites. Think of it like brushing your teeth: Sure, you can skip it, but you're absolutely inviting both short-term and long-term dental issues into your life. Harvesting your cocoons properly helps keep your managed bee population healthy and functional, like a quick brush helps keep your teeth healthy.

Harvesting cocoons also gives you a chance to share a bit of backyard science with young family members or neighbors; including a few celebratory snacks can transform it from a brief but boring solo task into a little bee-harvest festival. The precise date is flexible, but the general season of midfall (right around the time the apple harvest is in full swing in the northern half of the United States) is the perfect time to sort your cocoons for signs of disease and move them into colder storage for hibernation.

Harvest Methods

You will need a few basic, readily available tools on hand, depending on the type of nesting tubes or trays you used. Here is a list of what you need to acquire before the harvesting process:

- wooden skewer (for paper or cardboard tubes with backs)
- scissors to open nesting materials (for cardboard tubes)
- razor blade or well-sharpened paring knife (for paper tubes)
- reed splitter (for reeds)
- pliers (for reeds)
- needle-nose or jeweler's pliers (for inserts)
- bowl of water
- tongue depressors or a small measuring spoon
- slim slotted screwdriver

- Cocoon Comb (see Resources) or Phillips screwdriver for removing cocoons (for wood trays and natural reeds)
- old toothbrush or small, stiff wire brush to remove stuck-on debris (for wood trays)
- a couple of clean, dry, empty bowls or boxes

Paper and Cardboard Tube Harvest

Some mason bees abandon their hole without finishing the end of the hole with a thick plug of mud. To find all cocoons, it is best to check every nesting tube. If you used tubes with a solid back, your first step in harvesting may take a bit longer than if you used a style with a hole in the back. Since you cannot see to the end of the tube, you will need to use a long wooden skewer as a depth gauge to determine whether a mason bee used the tube. Insert the skewer into a completely empty tube and mark the depth of the tube on the skewer. Now use this gauge to measure the rest of your tubes. If the mark on the gauge is higher than the tube, a mason bee has probably left at least one cocoon chamber inside.

If you made your own paper nesting tubes or used purchased tubes with a small hole on the "closed" end, look through the end of each tube to see if it is empty. If you see light at the end, a mason bee has not used the tube. Set it aside and use it next season.

Next, check the mud plugs of completely filled nesting tubes for any holes. Then, examine along the length of the paper tube for holes. If you find any, it typically means that pests invaded your cocoons. Set these aside to examine further after you have finished sorting your healthy cocoons (see chapter 5 for a primer on mason bee pests).

Carefully tear or snip with scissors one end of the tube, and it will easily unravel. Gently use your fingers to separate mason bee cocoons from the paper.

Natural Reed Harvest

Using a desk lamp or the flashlight on your phone, look to see if there is light at the end of each reed. If you see light, a mason bee has not used the tube. Set it aside and use it next season.

A reed splitter is a specialty cutting tool (see Resources) that will save your fingers the effort of splitting through tougher reeds, larger reeds for wild bees, or thick bamboo segments. The concave bottom of the splitter holds reeds in place while the blade cuts the reed lengthwise at the node end. Cutting at the node reduces the risk of squishing cocoons near the mud-capped end. This tool will split the reed cleanly in half, making it easy to remove the cocoons by hand and examine the reed interior for signs of pests.

If you do not have a reed splitter, gently squeeze enough to crack the reed slightly at the

Crack the reed open on the mudded end with your fingers, then gently split it lengthwise to reveal the cocoons. (Dave Hunter/Crown Bees)

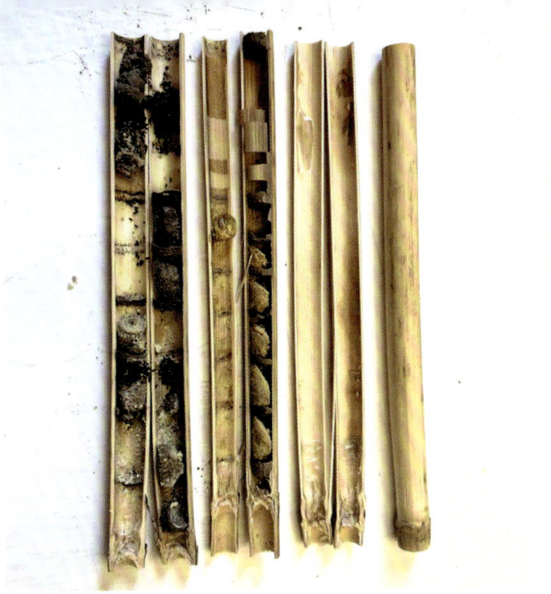

LEFT: *Split reed with cocoons in fall (left), pollen loaves and bee eggs (center), and an empty reed open and closed (right)* (Dave Hunter/Crown Bees) **RIGHT:** *If you use a tray-style bee house, make sure to clean it every fall.* (Dave Hunter/Crown Bees)

mud-sealed tip of the reed; it should now be easy to split. Another method is to crack the front of the reed with your fingers before gently squeezing and splitting the length of the reed. Reeds seem stiff and sturdy, but this simple twist-and-push technique will open them right up. Once it is split, use your fingers to pull the reed apart, then brush the cocoons out of either side with your fingers.

Wooden Tray Harvest

Remove the rubber bands and cardboard backing (save both to reassemble the trays) from the trays. Lift the first tray, and using a Cocoon Comb or Phillips screwdriver, gently remove all cocoons, leaf bits, and other debris. Keep your removal tool at a 45-degree angle to the tray to avoid damaging cocoons. Remember to check both sides of the trays.

To clean the trays for reusing next season, brush away any pollen and mason bee frass with an old toothbrush or another small, stiff brush. Next, gently clean all areas of each tray with a different small brush dipped in a bleach-and-water solution (1 tablespoon [15 milliliters] bleach to 1 cup [236 milliliters] water) to remove any chalkbrood that may be present. Dry the trays completely. Once they are clean and dry, reassemble the trays by aligning the side grooves. Double-check that the trays are snug and that there are no gaps between the tracks. Store the trays with the cardboard backing and rubber bands attached.

Cocoon Inspection and Cleaning

Now it is time to inspect the cocoons and see how successful your bees were as parents for the year. Gently place your healthy-looking cocoons in a clean, dry bowl or box. You should find nothing that is harmful to touch, although you might be surprised by an earwig or other creepy-crawly.

Distinct cocoon (left); undefined cocoon (right) (Dave Hunter/Crown Bees)

You should notice two types of cocoons:

- Defined cocoons: These represent 99 percent of cocoons, where the males are smaller and females are larger. You will likely see a bit of frass, or brown larva poop, on the outside of the cocoons. This is a good sign, not anything to worry about.
- Undefined cocoons: These look like wispy bits of cocoon silk, and you might even see something that looks like a bee inside. However, the cocoon is not a solid oval shape forming a complete protective layer; the bee inside chose not to spin a perfect cocoon. Because it is less than perfect, do not clean this cocoon, as you may damage the hibernating bee.

Everything else you encounter should fall into a few distinct categories: mud, leftover pollen balls, frass, an occasional cocoon with a hole in it, perhaps a big wiggly larva of a beneficial wasp, a thin cocoon with a mud plug that looks almost like a bullet (likely another type of wasp), or another kind of insect.

Why is there leftover pollen? Probably the mason bee forgot to lay an egg in the pollen mass, or the larva died before it was able to eat any of it. It might have been notably rainy when the mason bee gathered pollen (making the pollen mass too soupy), and the extra moisture caused the cocoon to become waterlogged, drowning the larva. There is nothing in particular that can be done about this occasional loss, as bees, pollen, and rain go hand in hand. But when you find a string of pollen balls in one hole, it is likely that that bee visited a bush or tree laden with chemicals, particularly a larvicide.

If all nesting holes are filled, you might find bees creating their own spot to create pollen/egg chambers. (Paula Arms)

It's possible a neighbor sprayed their trees while your bees were active; if you find a nesting hole with this pattern, have a conversation with your neighbors about how you can work together in the future.

Sometimes, one of your nesting tubes will have a mud plug with few to no cocoons behind it. Why? Toward the end of the mason bee's life, she can get a form of dementia. She knows she is supposed to cover holes with mud, and she will do that until she dies, even if an egg has not been laid in that hole. Again, there is nothing that can be done.

Storing Cleaned Cocoons

Clean mason bee cocoons should be stored in your refrigerator until the following spring. The consistent cold temperatures of your fridge help the mason bees conserve their fat stores over the winter. Set your fridge temperature between 34° and 38°F (1° and 3°C). Because modern frost-free refrigerators have reduced moisture levels, your cocoons may begin to dry out after a few weeks. To prevent cocoon dehydration, options include Crown Bee's HumidiBee Cocoon Humidifier. Adding about one tablespoon (15 milliliters) of water once each winter month to this humidifier keeps cocoons from drying out. You may also use any ventilated plastic box with a paper or thin foam liner.

Store your mason bee cocoons in the fridge over the winter. (Dave Hunter/Crown Bees)

Spores from cheese or foods past their prime are constantly circulating around your refrigerator and can sometimes cause mason bee cocoons to become moldy. You can often prevent spores from reaching your cocoons by placing their storage box in a paper bag. A little mold growth is not a big deal, but if the cocoons get excessively moldy, you can rewash them in cool water, pat dry, and (optionally) spritz with Crown Bees' Clean Bee (see Resources) to treat mold growth; you can also give them a preemptive spritz with this spray before refrigeration. If you are using a HumidiBee, rinse the liner pads in warm, soapy water; let dry; and evenly spritz Clean Bee on both sides of the pads. If you use a different box, wash and dry it thoroughly, and either replace or wash and dry the liner.

SPENDING TIME WITH YOUR MASON BEES

Spring can be a tremendously busy time in the garden. If you find yourself rushing to complete tasks without pausing for a moment to purely

BEE BUY BACK PROGRAM

Bee Buy Back is a simple program offered by Crown Bees. Harvest your cocoons in the fall, count them, calculate how many bees you want to keep for the following spring, and send the excess back to Crown Bees. The Bee Buy Back program opens at the beginning of October of each year and remains open until the quota is met. In return for your extra cocoons, you can receive a gift certificate or a credit for the amount earned. (See Resources for information on how to participate in this program.)

enjoy your space, your bees can provide reasons to take a beat and simply watch to see what these small creatures get up to over the course of a day.

Early Morning

Bees have their own version of "waking up with the sun." Mason bees need warmth more than light before they will shake their wings and roll out of bed for the day. If you are an early bird, pour yourself a cup of tea or coffee and sit near your bee house for 30 to 45 minutes as direct sun comes to rest on it. As the house warms up, you will see the bees come out of their holes one by one and sit among their neighbors as they continue to warm up, before buzzing off to begin their tasks for the day. It is not all that different from watching birds visit a feeder: You'll enjoy knowing they are up and about like you are, and if you've been working to attract wild mason bees, now is a fine opportunity to look for differences among your bees.

Midmorning to Midafternoon

You will notice that there are tasks that you will easily find your bees doing and other tasks that are trickier to spot. You are likely to find them crawling all over their favorite blossoms—their dark little bodies stand out starkly against pale flowers. Within a few minutes' watching, you will probably find one or two at their nesting holes, either returning with a bit of mud, pollen, or nectar, or flying away after depositing the most recent bundle. If you time it right, you can even catch a bee completing the final seal of mud on a filled nesting tube. And if it is your first year of keeping bees, chances are you will not be able to resist counting the filled tubes every day or two as you see them gradually increase. Truly, watching the bees live their busy little lives never gets old. Even after a few years of keeping bees, you will still notice curious details about these interesting creatures. The restful pleasure of it might distract you from doing your own chores!

Checking the bee house for filled nesting tubes is a fun task to do with kids, either your own or the budding scientist next door. A sealed-off tube is noticeable at a glance, and you can get right up close to count, noting as you do that the bees are going in and out of other tubes without even pausing to say hello.

This is also an easy time to look for obvious signs of other animals enjoying the bee house.

A mason bee visits a rosemary blossom. (Bill McLain)

An occasional spider might lay an egg sac, for example (which is not ideal because you would not want the front of your bee house covered in sticky spiderwebs; try moving it gently if you think you can), or you might see signs that a woodpecker is creeping near to dig out the bee larvae. That's your indication that it is time to put up a birdproof screen.

It is harder to spot the bees gathering their mud, mainly because you do not have the benefit of the color contrast of dark bees on pale flowers—and because getting a good view of mud might mean lying belly down on some damp ground for a while. If you can keep yourself comfortable, it is an amazing sight. The delicacy with which a mason bee plucks mud from your mud basin is remarkable—and worth a photo or two, if you are willing to lie down to get them. Bees on flowers? We're used to those pictures. Bees on mud is a much rarer shot to see shared on social media and a learning opportunity for your friends and family. Place a lawn

LEFT: *Your bees won't mind if you play paparazzi when you spot them at their front doors.* (Jill Lightner) **RIGHT:** *Notice the pollen grains on the bee's fuzzy face.* (Jill Lightner)

chair near the mud hole you created, and you will be able to comfortably watch them at their mud collection throughout the course of a day.

Late Afternoon to Early Evening

As the weather cools and the sun fades—how long this takes obviously varies depending on how far from the equator you live and how late in the season it is—you will see that your bees slowly withdraw into their tubes for the night. If you are not enough of an early riser to have caught them leaving their nest holes when they woke in the morning, spend a few minutes watching how they all return to rest up for the next busy day of pollen and mud collecting and egg laying. They tend to sleep with their heads facing out of the tube—and, like us, they might have different preferences for sleeping on their sides, bellies, or backs. If you aim a bright light into their tubes, you can spot their eyes.

CHAPTER 4

LEAF BEES: WHAT TO DO WHEN

The alfalfa leaf bee became a widely praised agricultural heroine after its introduction from Europe in the 1930s, when it saved North America's declining alfalfa harvest. Rapid industrialization of North American farming in the early 20th century led to dramatic habitat loss on newly cleared land. Critical wild pollinators were threatened, including many of the approximately 240 North American native leaf bee species. This in turn threatened a major source of food for livestock: high-protein alfalfa. Thanks to the gregarious nature of this leaf bee (making it willing to nest in shared housing boxes, like mason bees do), today it is used extensively to pollinate this key crop along with other summertime crops that are grown on a smaller scale, and it does not seem to have created a drastic negative impact on the hundreds of our native leaf bee species.

Because of their commercial uses, the leaf population is robust, but they are not widely known in home gardens, possibly because their most common name is "leafcutting bee," which reminds people of

LEFT: *More than 200 leafcutter bee species are native to North America.* (Dave Hunter/Crown Bees) **RIGHT:** *Leaf bees don't destroy your garden leaves the way some caterpillars do.* (bigemrg/iStock)

damaging caterpillar or locust infestations. Do not let that name inspire visions of your beautiful foliage plants being peppered with holes from these friendly and useful bees. The minor cuts that leaf bees make in leaves do not harm the plants. Particularly when you're growing annual bean and pea crops, getting a larger harvest in exchange for the bees snipping what they need from the leaves will be a worthwhile trade. Bees and flowering plants have evolved together for millions of years, in a mutual relationship. Bees get food and nesting materials from the plants, and in return, the plants use bees to carry pollen to other plants of the same species. Both species win! Some people find the cuts unsightly, but we prefer to think of them as evidence of pollination in action and a sign of a thriving garden ecosystem.

These small, gentle bees are a fantastic garden addition for anyone who raises melons, tomatoes, squash, beans, eggplant, late-season berries, and other hot-weather food crops or later-season orchard crops such as persimmon and Asian pear. If daytime temperatures are at least 75°F (21°C) when your edible crops are blossoming, leaf bees are likely a better pollinator choice than mason bees.

Leaf bees focus on pollen and nectar as a food supply for themselves and their eggs, using the small, circular snips of leaf only to surround the pollen cavity and close off the walls between the eggs they lay, totaling about one small leaf each day a bee is active. Compared with caterpillars that use leaves both as their primary diet and as a nesting spot on which to spin their cocoons, leaf bees' effects are almost unnoticeable, while the benefit to fruit and vegetable harvests is obvious. If she cannot find the right type of leaf to cut and carry in her legs to the nest, a bee will leave your yard and set up her home elsewhere. It takes only a couple of hours of effort each year to keep leaf bees, but you do need to time those hours correctly across the four seasons for success.

Remember that the pollinating lifespan of a leaf bee is only four to six weeks; their time spent buzzing about your garden is only as long as your hot-weather food crops are blooming. The process for placing out leaf cocoons is the same as for mason bees, but it is later in the season (see Table 4-1), and the bees are a little smaller, with no size differentiations between the male and female cocoons. If you keep both mason and leaf bees, remove the filled mason bee tubes for summer protection from parasites in the first half of June, and place out smaller tubes, reeds, or wooden trays for leaf bees. Once again, the males will hatch first, find some nearby pollen, and hover near the house, waiting for females to emerge.

TABLE 4.1. LEAF BEE CARE TIMELINE

DAYTIME TEMPERATURE	WHAT TO DO
Mid-April	Harvest all cocoons.
One month before temperatures are predicted to hit 80°F	Move half of the cocoons into a warm environment, out of direct sunlight and protected from birds; a cocoon hatchery tube (see Resources) can help.
One week later	Move the remainder of the cocoons into a warm environment, out of direct sunlight and protected from birds; a cocoon hatchery tube (see Resources) can help.
80°F (27°C), week 1	Release the first half of the cocoons.
80°F, week 3	Release the remaining half of the cocoons.
Labor Day/Fête du Travail	Collect all nesting tubes. Keep them outside (or in a shed) in a breathable, transparent bag, out of direct sunlight.

There is no need to cut leaves and bring them to the bees. Cut leaves quickly wilt, and human scissors will do more harm to the plant than the snips from a leaf bee. The right leaves are vital, and as long as there is a reliable source within 100 feet (30 meters) of the nesting tubes or trays, your bees will have no trouble finding and cutting what they need.

Leaf bees tend to disperse more readily than mason bees; if you plan to keep both species, you'll notice that we suggest a greater number of leaf cocoons when first getting started. These numbers mean you will end up with a good number of bees that remain to pollinate your plants even after a percentage buzzes off to a different garden. Because one leaf bee can potentially create up to 35 cocoons each year,[1] every year, the number of bees should grow naturally for the following year. This year's bees are laying next year's bees; you should expect to at least double your bee population annually, at a bare minimum. If all goes as intended for your leaf bees, you can dramatically boost the number of pollinators in your neighborhood each year. As your bee population grows, you need to make sure you have the right number of nesting holes; this is the second step in your annual inventory process. If you are starting with 20 cocoons, you will need 30 to 40 straws, tubes, or holes (as described in chapter 2), or about two holes per cocoon. If this is the first year you are keeping leaf bees, you can order your bee cocoons online to be shipped to you at the right time for setting outside in your specific environment, much like when you order nursery plants (see Resources).

After a year or two of managing your own leaf bee population, you'll almost certainly have cocoons to share. We encourage you to find as direct a connection as possible to pass along cocoons, including advice on nesting materials and gardening practices as needed. Offer them to neighbors, work colleagues, community gardens, or garden clubs, or find homes for them online via a nearby Buy Nothing group

SEASONAL ALERT!

If you also keep mason bees, the end of winter and the beginning of spring is when you should be placing out your cocoons. Refer to chapter 3 for the correct temperatures and schedule.

(download the free app or look for group pages on social media) or through Craigslist or similar forums. Aside from providing a nudge in the direction of bee-friendly gardening practices, sharing cocoons helps build a sense of community among solitary beekeepers, increase bees' popularity, and increase the population of pollinators, a benefit to us all.

WINTER: COOL AND COZY STORAGE

Other than occasionally checking in on your stored leaf cocoons, winter is downtime for leaf bees and their keepers. The main thing you'll want to do for leaf bees in this season is to make sure your garden will be a healthy and welcoming place for midsummer bees. Do you have the correct plants in mind, and are you prepared to avoid unfriendly chemicals? Are you set for a fresh supply of nesting materials if you use paper or cardboard tubes or natural reeds?

Leaf bees, which overwinter in a pupa stage, do best if stored in an unheated garage or shed for the season, away from windows. While you will want to keep your leaf bees cool, the refrigerator is not a good option for them. The leaves get moldy easily in a refrigerator, and it is hard to eliminate the mold without harming the bees. Leaf bees will not begin to develop into adult bees until the temperatures are 60–70°F (15.5–21°C). Most nonheated spaces are cooler than that through the winter.

SPRING: HARVEST TIME

Harvesting significantly reduces the incidences of pests, parasites, and diseases and allows managed bees to thrive year after year. Don't panic if you spot anything that seems concerning. Many parasites are native predators that evolved alongside leaf bees and thus are common. But that doesn't mean we have to allow them to feast on our bees! You'll want to harvest your leaf bees in early spring, right around the time that dandelions are blooming where you live.

LEFT TO RIGHT: *Leaf bee larva, leaf bee mid-development, leaf bee female* (Alan Anderson USDA ARS Pollinating Insects Research Unit)

YOU BETTER BEE-LEAF IT! TOP 10 LEAVES FOR LEAF BEES

Not any leaf will do. Soft, flexible, nonfibrous leaves are right for a leaf bee's purposes. These leaves are thin but sturdy, without too many veins. Thicker leaves from azaleas or camellias, for example, are too tough, while lettuces, or leaves from thin-leaved trees like birches, tend to be packed with fibrous little veins. A few leafy plants are plenty to support hundreds of nesting females. If your garden space doesn't include one of these plants, borrow a leaf from a friend or favorite garden center to use for comparison to make sure that you have something nearly identical.

- alfalfa
- rose
- lilac
- peas of all types
- beans of all types
- asters
- redbud trees
- sunflowers
- clover of all types
- hostas

Harvesting can be a bit messy, because crumbly bits of leaves will fall off the cocoons. We suggest wearing gardening clothes that you're comfortable working in and laying down newspaper or an old sheet to make cleaning up easier. Almost everything will be contained inside the leafy chambers, but you may find pollen loaves from bee eggs that never hatched, and possibly dead leaf bee larvae, along with pests such as chalkbrood, pollen mites, or other parasites. The combination makes harvesting a fascinating but fairly messy process.

In general, you will find the leafy sections all in a neat row. When you pick these sections up, they will naturally break into smaller, fairly fragile, leaf-surrounded cocoons. Surprisingly, most of the pests are hidden within the leaf bits, unseen. Leaf bee pests tend to lay their eggs within the pollen and overwinter as the leaf bees do, as larvae encased in leaves. Leaf bee cocoons are not waterproof. Never wash leaf bee cocoons!

Leaf bees concealed in a leafy embrace (Dave Hunter/Crown Bees)

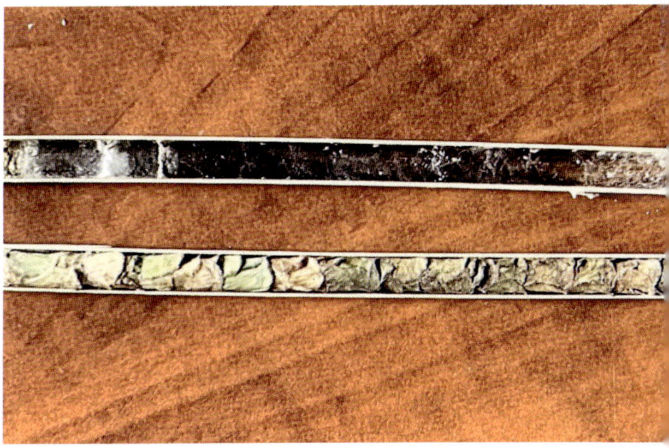

HOW MANY LEAF BEES FOR MY SPACE?

- 100 leaf bee cocoons for a 200-square-foot (18.5-square-meter) balcony with vegetable and flower containers
- 200 leaf bee cocoons for a 2,500-square-foot (232-square-meter) yard with vegetable and flower beds
- 400 leaf bee cocoons for a 1/4-acre (0.1-hectare) yard with vegetable and flower beds
- 1,000 leaf bee cocoons for a 1-acre (0.4-hectare) community garden
- Want to bring leaf bees to Shiloh Field Community Garden, the largest of its kind in the United States? You'd need around 8,000 cocoons for its 14.5-acre (5.6-hectare) space.

Recommended harvesting tools include:

- Cocoon Comb (see Resources) or Phillips screwdriver for removing cocoons (for wood trays and natural reeds)
- BeeGuard Bag (see Resources) or another breathable, transparent bag for leaf bee incubation
- old toothbrush or small, stiff wire brush to remove stuck-on debris (for wood trays)
- scissors to open nesting materials (for cardboard BeeTubes)
- reed splitter or pliers (for natural reeds)

Wood Tray Harvest

Remove the rubber bands, cardboard backing, and pest blocker (save everything to reassemble the trays). Lift the first tray, and using a Cocoon Comb or Phillips screwdriver, gently remove all cocoons, leaf bits, and other debris. Keep your removal tool at a 45-degree angle to the tray to avoid damaging cocoons. Remember to check both sides of the trays!

To clean the trays for reusing next season, brush away any pollen and leaf bee frass with an old toothbrush or small, stiff brush. Next, gently clean all areas of each tray with a different small brush dipped in a bleach-and-water solution (1 tablespoon [15 milliliters] bleach to 1 cup [236 milliliters] water) to remove any chalkbrood that may be present. Dry the trays completely. Once they are clean and dry, reassemble the trays by aligning the side grooves. Double-check that the trays are snug and that there are no gaps between the tracks. Store the trays with the cardboard backing, pest blocker, and rubber bands attached.

Natural Reed Harvest

A reed splitter is a specialty cutting tool (see Resources) that will save your fingers the effort of splitting through tough reeds as well as larger natural reeds used for wild bees and thick bamboo segments. The concave bottom of the splitter holds reeds in place while the blade cuts the reed lengthwise at the node end. Cutting at the node reduces the risk of squishing cocoons near the mud-capped end. This tool will split the reed cleanly in half, making it easy to remove the cocoons by hand and examine the interior for signs of pests.

If you do not have a reed splitter, gently squeeze the reed just enough to crack it slightly at the mud-sealed tip; it should now be easy to split. Pinch the leaf-capped end between your fingers or a pair of pliers, until the reed starts to split. You typically will not find a cocoon at the open end of the reed.

An easier method is to find a reed splitter (see Resources) and cut through the back end of the reed (node side). Once you have cut through the node, simply twist the splitter and the reed will open up down the middle.

Once the reed is split open, use your fingers to pull it apart, then brush the cocoons out of either side with a Cocoon Comb, a Phillips screwdriver, or your fingers. The opened and emptied reeds can go into the yard waste or compost bin.

Leafcutter bees during incubation (Dave Hunter/ Crown Bees)

Cardboard BeeTube Harvest

Tear or carefully snip with scissors one end of the BeeTube, and it will easily unravel. Gently use your fingers to separate leaf bee cocoons from the paper. Don't place the tubes in water to dissolve the glue, as these cocoons aren't waterproof.

STORING LEAF BEE COCOONS

Now that you have harvested the leaf cocoons, they are vulnerable to ants, wasps, and other predators. Crown Bees makes a bag called a BeeGuard, from industrial-strength organza with double drawstring closures. The material is a strong, fine mesh that allows good ventilation but prevents pests from getting in easily. A similar option is the 941.08 Wasp-Proof Storage Bag from Beediverse (see Resources), made of finely woven mesh and closed with heavy drawstrings. If you prefer a DIY project, heavy-duty organza is available at some specialty fabric stores and can be stitched or glued into a similar nesting tube armor bag. The size should loosely accommodate your clean cocoons and close securely enough that tiny predators cannot get inside. Drawstrings are better than Velcro,

PEST PATROL

Concerned about what you're finding with your cocoons? Refer to the following sections to identify and manage leaf bee pests

- chalkbrood fungus, page 89
- *Pteromalus venustus*, page 93
- Sapygidae (sapygid or club-horned) wasps, page 93
- moth and beetle larvae, page 94

ATTRACTING WILD LEAF BEES

While the alfalfa leaf bee is an introduced species that is well established across the continent, many other leaf bees are native to North America from Florida up to Canada. Instead of purchasing your first set of cocoons, you may prefer to try to attract some of these wild bees and give them a clean and healthy home. While not always successful, combining a pheromone spray (a scent attractant) with a few natural reeds (a visual attractant) is a good strategy to attract wild bees. Both components are available online (see Resources) and at some garden nurseries. Spray the reeds and tuck them into a bee house (even if your other nesting tubes are a different material, you should be able to add a few reeds).

Expect wild bees to vary in size more than purchased bees, and the sizes of their nesting tubes need to vary more too. To best support wild bees, offering a range of nesting tube diameters from 5/32 inch (4 millimeters) to ⅜ inch (10 millimeters) is a good idea, with a depth of 6 inches (15.25 centimeters).

as it is difficult to seal the ends of a Velcro strip, and ants and tiny wasps can crawl into the bag through these almost invisible gaps. Store the bag of leaf bee cocoons in your garage or shed until it's time for summer incubation.

You can use a leaf bee incubator to ensure the right amount of heat and humidity. (Dave Hunter/Crown Bees)

SUMMER: LEAF BEE INCUBATION AND EMERGENCE

Leaf bees hibernate within their leafy cocoons as larvae and need strong heat with no direct sun to develop into adult bees. You will want to keep the leaf cocoons in a warm, dark place for many weeks before you plan on bees flying around your garden. Incubation can happen indoors or out, because it's the heat that they need, not the sunshine. A warm garage shelf or cupboard will suit them, as will a shady part of a greenhouse or potting shed. Remember, no direct sunlight on the cocoons!

Leaf bees like weather that is substantially warmer than what is needed by early spring's mason bees. Time your leaf bee emergence with your summer weather and coinciding open blooms. The warmer the temperatures, the faster bees develop into adults. At 84°F (30°C), adults emerge after about three weeks, or 20 days. In a cooler region, or simply a cooler year, it can take considerably longer. At 70°F (21°C), adults emerge after about six weeks, or 42 days. Humidity is also key: Below 30 percent daily

LEFT: *Plant peas, beans, or strawberries around the same time you start incubating leafcutter cocoons.* (Jill Lightner) **RIGHT:** *A leaf bee emerging into the world* (Dave Hunter/Crown Bees)

humidity, they will dry out and not develop and emerge.

It is possible for leaf bees to have multiple seasons in one summer. If temperatures allow, in the realm of 85°F (29°C), a bee that should be in her larval stage to emerge the following year may develop immediately into a full-fledged bee. She'll move through any larvae in front of her in the same tube, killing them in the process. While this is natural, the best way to prevent this from occurring is to know when a reed or tube has been completed and remove it from the warm bee house and place it in cooler storage.

Your bee house may have attracted some native leaf bees last season. Some species of leaf bees have shorter development cycles than others and will emerge earlier, making it a good idea to check the bag periodically. Release any early emergers near your bee house in the morning. Once adult leaf bees start to emerge, release cocoons by placing them into a cocoon hatchery or similar container and then placing that container in or near your bee house.

How should you time the cocoon release? Match them to the blossoms they'll be pollinating. Plants grow quickly in summer's heat, and unless you have a truly remarkable variety of berries, beans, melons, and squash, chances are that their bloom times are fairly close together. To match this short bloom time, you may want to place leaf cocoons out in intervals that are accordingly close together. If you set out half your leaf bees around mid-June and the other half about two weeks later, your summer food garden should be well covered.

HEAT WARNING!

Intact cocoons can't regulate their temperatures above 90°F (32°C); if your storage area gets above that during the incubation period, bring the cocoons to a cooler location, like indoors, and release adult bees in the early morning as they emerge until the weather cools.

SMOKEY BEAR IS A FRIEND TO BEES

For years, wildfire smoke was an occasional West Coast problem, but that is no longer the case. Fires now affect air quality across North America differently each year, and depending on where you live, weather conditions, and human errors, the dreaded smoke season can occur anywhere from May to October. It's tough to determine precisely how air quality that can harm humans impacts managed solitary bees, although a two-year study at Oregon State University led by forest wildlife ecologist Jim Rivers found that robust, highly diverse populations of wild bees are found in higher numbers in regions recovering from severe fires when compared to milder fires—likely because tree loss creates more sunshine for abundant flowering plants.[2]

In 2020, when Oregon experienced its worst fires in state history up to that point, the Oregon State Extension Service explained that bees and many insects use polarized light patterns as maps between their nests and flowers. Clouds do not distort these patterns, but the haze in smoke-filled skies does. It appears that not only do bees' maps get difficult for them to read, but also the pattern map can shift, making a bee think her flower bed or nesting cavity is in the wrong place. Navigation between two essential points suddenly becomes impossible—and depending on the timing of the smoke and haze, it can extend over the entire short life of a bee.

Most of us do not fight fires ourselves or have superhero-like abilities to repair polarized light directions, so what can we do? In the United States, an estimated 85 percent of wildfires are caused by human behavior, and in Canada, the estimate is 50 percent. We can all do something about these events. Check in with your pal Smokey Bear at Smokeybear.com for the most recent advice, but the basics haven't changed in decades: Respect burn bans, do not light fireworks, learn the correct (and somewhat tedious, but thorough!) method to genuinely smother a campfire, and beware of even a single spark from gas-powered vehicles and equipment anywhere near dry plants.

Releasing leaf bee cocoons means placing cocoons into your bee house so they can emerge and begin summer activities; a cocoon hatchery tube or tray may be useful (see Resources). Leaf bees emerge from their cocoons as fully mature bees. Females often return to where they emerged and search for a nearby nesting cavity to lay their eggs. This behavior is why bee raisers release their leaf bee cocoons inside or near their bee house—it increases the likelihood the females will choose to nest in the provided house. You can also use the same pheromone spray used to attract wild leaf bees (see Resources).

Leaf bees can remain actively pollinating and nesting through mid-August, so for their health it is important to continue avoiding unfriendly chemicals. Weeding by hand, letting clover grow, and managing pests by hand removal or a bit of salt, dish soap, or vinegar spray (see chapter 5) are the safest techniques to keep your pollinators thriving. Additionally, midsummer is when wild pollinators are most active (bumble bees of all sizes are particularly noticeable; see Table 1.1), and you do not want to cause them problems either.

FALL: STORAGE SEASON

When temperatures cool to 60°F (15°C), leaf bees will have completed nesting for the season. Leaf bees hibernate as delicate larvae inside their leafy cocoons over the fall and winter. So, to protect them from pests, you'll want to remove, protect, and store the nesting materials to keep the hibernating larvae safe from parasitic wasps, ants, birds, and other predators. Storage for leaf bees is notably different from storage for mason bees, partly because of life cycle differences and partly because of temperature requirements. Unlike mason bees, you do not sort the cocoons at this time, nor should you store leaf bee nesting material in the refrigerator.

Leaf bee larvae take about 20 days to consume their pollen loaf, then begin spinning their silk cocoons. (Mary Holland)

Remove

Leaf bees typically complete nesting by late summer or early fall, depending on temperatures. Once you no longer see females moving

Some of the pollen carried by leaf bees' fuzzy bodies is spread to other flowers, and some is taken back for egg laying. (Dave Hunter/Crown Bees)

Filled leaf bee trays; note the varied color petals gathered for their end caps! (Dave Hunter/Crown Bees)

in and out of your bee house, or daytime temps drop to 60°F (15°C), it's time to remove the filled nesting materials.

For wood trays, remove the entire set of trays as a single unit.

For natural reeds or BeeTubes, it is possible to remove filled, individual nesting tubes as soon as you see the leaf-capped end, but we do not recommend it automatically because leaf bees use visual cues to locate their nests. If you shift their nesting materials around, the females may become disoriented and abandon the nests. For this reason, we don't recommend removing individually filled nesting materials unless there is evidence of predators or the temperatures are consistently in the range of 90°F (32°C; see Heat Warning!, page 79, for explanation).

If you decide to remove filled tubes, replace each filled tube with a fresh, empty tube in its spot, so active females will be able to locate their specific nests. We also recommend you swap the tubes in the evenings to help females reorient to

BEWARE THE BIRDS!

Birds are a joy to have in your yard, but you don't have to allow them to treat your bee house like an all-you-can-eat buffet, something that woodpeckers and some jays would love to do. You can make a bird deterrent screen with a panel of ¾-inch (2-centimeter) galvanized wire mesh; wire-mesh squares of this size don't impact bee access but make the cocoons considerably more difficult for hungry birds to eat. When you install the mesh, create a 2-inch (5-centimeter) bubble around the front of the house rather than installing it flush with the nesting material, as this could prevent bees from reaching their nests. Crown Bees also offers Bird Guard panels cut to fit your specific bee house (see Resources). Sometimes, the bee house has something like an empty attic at the top, which could appeal to small birds looking for nesting cavities. Filling the space with rocks or covering it with more galvanized mesh will deter them.

any minor changes when they begin flying again in the morning.

Protect

Place all filled nesting materials into the same BeeGuard Bag (or other breathable, transparent bag) that you use to store the cleaned cocoons in spring, making sure to place filled nesting tubes with their leafy-capped ends face up. The bag will protect the developing bees from hungry predators, and placing the leafy-capped ends face up will help ensure the egg and developing bee stay on top of the pollen loaf (bee food).

If rodents are an issue where you'll store the cocoons, place nesting materials into a thick plastic or metal chew-proof container. Make sure to add a few air holes to the container.

Store

The development of leaf bees is temperature dependent, so make sure you store the bag in a dry area with temperatures that are cooler than outdoors, such as an unheated garage or shed, until harvest time the following spring. If they must remain outside, protect them from rain, snow, and predators. Regularly check the storage bag for the first few weeks and look for any parasites that may have emerged; you should kill any pests and parasites to keep them from attacking your developing bees. Checking them at this stage should reduce problems when you clean and separate leaf cocoons in the spring.

SPENDING TIME WITH YOUR LEAF BEES

In contrast to mason bees' often-rainy spring season, peak leaf bee time coincides with the longest days of the year, kids' summer vacations, and the joys of "summer Fridays" for some lucky adults. As you enjoy—or occasionally grumble

A leaf bee returns to the nesting tube with a piece of honeysuckle leaf. (Andi Edwards/istock)

over—your garden chores or host your friends and family for a cookout, you'll have numerous opportunities to watch leaf queens buzzing about, see how they pollinate up close, and even witness them snipping their preferred leaves. First-time visitors may be anxious about stings, but you'll be able to address their concerns while acting as a leaf bee ambassador.

Early Morning

If you think you're living your best life when you're stretched out in a sunbeam, you have at least one thing in common with your leaf bees. On summer mornings, as their house gets warmer, you will see each bee come out of her nesting hole and sit with her neighbors as she wakes up. Take the opportunity to sit and

DR. THERESA SINGER

RESEARCH ENTOMOLOGIST

Dr. Theresa Singer retired in 2023 from her position as a research entomologist at the USDA Agricultural Research Service Pollinating Insects Research Unit in Logan, Utah. Her work with alfalfa leafcutter bees (referred to as "leaf bees" in this book) and blue orchard bees emphasized sustaining their populations and improving the management of the species for farmers across the American West. After more than two decades of work, her admiration for alfalfa leafcutter bees is clear, as she explained in an email: "The [alfalfa leafcutter bees] are very important pollinators for alfalfa seed production in western North America. The bees are extremely interesting to observe, are ferociously determined to build their nests, and are easy to rear and manipulate for experiments. The solitary bees offer a different look at bee versatility and ingenuity than do the social honey bees and bumble bees." Her experience working toward agricultural improvements with alfalfa crop management and the role played by bees creates a true partnership with the farmers, as she wrote, "It was important for me to understand their challenges, needs, and limitations so that my work had relevance. [Alfalfa seed producers] care a lot about their bees because they must have them for profitable yields and they often raise them on their farms. They are very serious and knowledgeable about their production operations, so they want solid and useful facts that take science and put it to practical use."

Dr. Singer provides a succinct reminder of how globally fundamental solitary bee species are and how difficult it can be to fight against widespread clichés about queen bees and hive minds: "I wish people would realize that not all bees live in colonies like honey bees and bumble bees. Most of the other ~25,000 species of bees globally are solitary or only somewhat social and live in the ground. Also, just because the social bees are more well-known and more widely produced as commercial pollinators does not mean that they are somehow inherently better or 'smarter' than the other bees." She also offers a memorable detail that backyard beekeepers can pass along to family and neighbors when they ask about bees: "A bee's brain grows as it matures as an adult. It learns from its experiences."

One fascinating insight from her research concerns how alfalfa leafcutter bees recognize their particular nests in enormous commercial bee boards that contain 3,540 separate nesting holes—it's not only about scent, but about the source of it: "My colleagues and I used high-powered microscopy and gas chromatography to reveal that the nest recognition chemicals are products of a gland that is associated with the bee's stinger." And something for you to take to heart: Alfalfa leafcutter bees are drawn to legume pollen, and clover is a legume present to some degree in almost every garden—for free. Letting it grow will give your bees exactly what they want in a food and nesting material source.

watch as you sip your morning beverage. You'll appreciate knowing they are up and about like you are.

Midmorning to Midafternoon

Depending on what vegetables and berry bushes are flowering in your garden, you may easily spot your leaf bees on clover or raspberry blooms or only as they fly in or out of deep zucchini or winter squash flowers. While they can be harder to spot procuring leaf pieces, pull up a chair near your roses or lilacs, and with a little patience, you'll witness them snipping leaves.

Switch your attention to their bee house and you will probably find one or two working on their nesting holes, or perhaps you'll notice additions to your count of filled tubes. The simple pleasure of observing your leaf bees can be calming or spark your curiosity. For example, some females drop the leaf they're carrying and instead of picking it up, off they go for a newly cut piece. Is it that it's too hard to find again, or was something wrong with the leaf?

If you have kids (or curious neighbor kids), have them assist you in checking the bee house for filled nesting tubes. A sealed-off tube is

A leaf bee can finish about two nesting holes in her six-week life. (Dave Hunter/Crown Bees)

immediately noticeable, and you can get up close to count them.

This is also an easy time to look for signs of other animals interacting with the bee house. A spider might lay an egg sac, for example (move it gently, if possible, as you do not want your bee house engulfed in webs). You might also see signs that a woodpecker is attempting to dig out the bee larvae. That's your indication that it is time to put up a Bird Guard screen (see Resources).

Late Afternoon to Early Evening

As the sun sets—of course, this varies depending on how far from the equator you live—you will see that your bees tuck in for the evening much the same way they rose in the morning, slowly withdrawing into their tubes as temperatures decrease. If you missed them at the start of their day, watch to see how they tuck themselves in for the night. They typically will be facing outward, so you can admire their little pollen-dusted faces as they sleep.

CHAPTER 5

PESTS AND THEIR BEE-FRIENDLY REMEDIES

Home gardeners have been conditioned to panic about pests for several generations, and it's past time to reconsider any "off with their heads!" reaction you may have about them. Ecosystems function as a whole—your bees will live their lives in your gardening spaces and perhaps those of your closest neighbors, surrounded by and interdependent with all sorts of other species that may occasionally earn the title of pest. A properly balanced ecosystem can seem like a theoretical ideal, but the general concept of plants and wildlife coexisting with minimal care from humans is worth investigating. Primarily, it's about working with nature rather than against it.

You may have heard the joke about a weed being a plant growing where we don't want it. Similarly, a pest can be a disease, fungus, parasite, predator, or living condition where you don't want it—or possibly something

TOP: *A mason bee with pollen mites* (Martin Dollenkamp/Frog Pond Photography) **BOTTOM:** *Pollen mites devour the bee bread, killing the mason bee egg. If the tube isn't cleaned, the following year they easily spread throughout the nesting tube.* (Dave Hunter/Crown Bees)

that can drastically and negatively impact the life of your bees or the plants they need to thrive. Because human-created treatments for such things can greatly impact the health of your bees—and your garden as an ecosystem—it makes sense to examine bee-specific concerns and broader plant concerns together, as part of the whole.

SOLITARY BEE PESTS AND THEIR REMEDIES

In the wild, the nesting holes of mason and leaf bees tend to be spread apart with some distance between them, and the majority of pests have a tough time moving from one hole to the next. Solitary bee houses created by humans concentrate a large amount of food into one delicious buffet for many different species, and control of these pests is the primary reason you must harvest both mason and leaf bee cocoons. If you let them self-manage without annual cleaning, it's easy to spread a handful of serious pests throughout your bee house and over to your neighbors—like what would happen to humans if hotels never changed the sheets. We want our bees to thrive, not merely survive. The more healthy bees we can produce, the better the yield for our fruits and plants. In most cases, a few pests are fine, but some need closer attention.

Pollen Mite

Affects: mason bees

Pollen mites look like fine-grained orange sawdust between some of the partitions in a nesting hole. Seen under magnification, the mites are clear and pink, and that orange dust is their feces. The mites are typically white, yellow, or red and are at first difficult to pick out from individual pollen grains when you view an infested nest. But, if you shake out the contents of the nest, you'll be able to see the mites move around. They are found throughout North America and tend to thrive in locations with a moist, humid environment. Their role in life is to consume leftover pollen in our flowers. Potentially there are bugs that prey on these pollen mites as well in the food chain. The symbiotic relationship bees have with pollen mites is that the bees allow mites to survive nicely in a protected hole through the winter. When fresh pollen is available, the bees bring back adult mites to the flowers to begin life again in your yard. You cannot prevent pollen mites from hitchhiking with the pollen that bees bring back to their nests, but you can remove them and keep their population in check.

Chalkbrood is a spore that can spread through mason bee holes if the cocoons aren't harvested. (Dave Hunter/Crown Bees)

What to do:

1. Do not reuse nesting tubes because pollen mites can easily spread. Clean reusable wood trays each season.
2. When harvesting mason bee cocoons in the fall, keep an eye out for signs of pollen mites. Harvesting mason bee cocoons is the easiest and best way to reduce pollen mite infections.

Chalkbrood Fungus

Affects: mason and leaf bees

The fungal pathogen called chalkbrood is highly destructive to cavity-nesting bees, and you should treat it as a high priority. There are many species, but each one affects specific types of bees. Adult bees are not affected, but they help spread it! Adult bees pick up chalkbrood from flowers and transfer spores to bee larvae during nest building. As the eggs hatch, bee larvae consume infected pollen, and the spores germinate in the larvae's gut. Chalkbrood then competes with the larvae for additional food, and the larvae starve and die, at which point the fungus keeps growing on carcasses. The following spring, as they exit the nesting tube, emerging adult bees pick up spores from these dead larvae, carrying them off to flowers and the new generation of bees. Two or three years of this can wipe out your bees. The spore-crusted larva carcass is chalky and breaks apart easily. The surface feels like the wing of a butterfly and tends to be dark gray.

What to do:

1. Only use nesting materials that allow you to open, inspect, and harvest cocoons.
2. Every year, be sure to follow the harvesting, cleaning, and sorting steps laid out for mason bees (chapter 3) and leaf bees (chapter 4). If you spot any chalkbrood cadavers, throw them away. Be extremely careful to avoid bringing healthy cocoons in contact with chalkbrood—spores are too tiny for you to see.
3. If you have found evidence of chalkbrood, wash mason bee cocoons with cool water, pat dry, and spritz with our Clean Bee solution, a safe bleach alternative. Alternatively, you

TOP: *Invasive species like the tiny Houdini fly have no predators and spread easily. The source of them is typically a neighbor who doesn't know to harvest their cocoons in the fall.* (Tomasz Klejdysz/iStock)
BOTTOM: *About twelve eggs are laid by a fly in each pollen mass. They quickly hatch and consume the pollen, remaining as maggots until the following spring.* (Dave Hunter/Crown Bees)

could wash mason bee cocoons with cool water-and-bleach solution (1 teaspoon [5 milliliters] bleach to 1 cup [237 milliliters] water), rinse with water, and pat them dry.

4. Nesting materials must be either cleaned with the same mild bleach solution or replaced before the following season. Rinse and dry materials well and allow the smell of bleach to dissipate. Wooden trays can warp as they dry, so once they have been cleaned, immediately band them tightly back together.

Houdini Fly

Affects: mason bees

First reported in New York in 2011, Houdini flies have been confirmed in many parts of North America in recent years. They're spreading mostly because of people sending unopened nesting material through the mail, and gardeners not opening their nesting holes to harvest in the fall. Broadly speaking, the largest vector is your neighbor.

Named after its unique method of escaping from bee nests, Houdini flies lay their eggs in nest cells before the female bee can seal the nest. The fly larvae quickly hatch and consume the pollen loaf before the bee larvae can, which causes the bees to starve. The Houdini larvae sit in the mason bee egg chamber through the summer, fall, and winter, developing into juveniles early in spring. Using its hydraulic head, a fly pushes into a crack and expands its head, which can chip out a piece of mud wall. Using this technique, they are able to almost magically escape their chamber. These parasites have large, red eyes and are slightly larger than a fruit fly (and much smaller than a house fly).

What to do:

1. Only use nesting materials that allow you to open, inspect, and harvest cocoons.
2. Harvest mason bee cocoons every fall. Open nesting materials and kill Houdini fly larvae (a garbage disposal is best; do not add them to a compost bin). Larvae look like sticky

white maggots inside the brood cell, often surrounded by curly orange/brown frass (poop).

3. Control adult bee emergence. If you cannot open nesting materials, or you skipped a year, place your nesting materials in a BeeGuard Bag or another fine mesh bag and close tightly. As bees emerge, release them daily and kill any adult Houdini flies.
4. Instantly kill any adult Houdini flies you see hovering around your bee house—they can be smooshed with your fingers on cooler mornings when they're moving slowly. Some bee raisers have noticed that regularly using a low-powered vacuum to remove Houdini flies from nesting materials can significantly reduce their numbers. Or mist them with water so they can't fly, before smooshing or vacuuming. Whichever technique you prefer, do it frequently for best results.
5. Before purchasing mason bees, ask the provider how they were harvested and whether they inspected the cocoons for Houdini flies. Do not purchase or accept unopened nesting material from friends or online shops. If you spot an untended mason bee box in your neighborhood, talk to its owner about Houdini flies and offer to clean, remove, or replace the box—it's likely home to a thriving collection of these parasites.

LONG-TERM PLANNING

Crown Bee has been heavily involved in research around the Houdini fly, working with multiple groups within the USDA. More studies are forthcoming, but we soon hope to provide specific, actionable information on protection against Houdini fly, as well as their management, for both gardeners and agriculturalists across North America.

Parasitic wasps are one of the most abundant life-forms on the planet, found wherever any insect exists. In 2023, the Natural History Museum of London added more than 600 parasitic wasps to their catalog, leading to nerdy, wasp-centered headlines from the British Broadcasting Corporation, National Public Radio, and science writer Sabrina Imbler in their column for Defector.com. Backyard beekeepers should expect some parasitic wasp sightings in their gardens, and it's definitely worth learning the differences among the most common.

Monodontomerus (Mono) Chalcid Wasp

Affects: mason bees

Chalcid wasps can be highly destructive parasites. The North American native *Monodontomerus* invades mason bee nests through small openings or weak spots in the nesting materials or through incomplete or uncapped nesting holes. They use their needlelike ovipositor (egg-laying tube) to paralyze bee larvae by inserting it through the side walls of bee nesting material, near the larvae. Female mono wasps can attack multiple bee cocoons. After paralyzing the bee larva, the female can lay up to several dozen eggs inside the cocoon. Upon hatching, the wasp larva consumes the bee and

TOP: *If mason bees are left unprotected in the summer, parasitic wasps , such as this mono wasp, can devastate them.* (Dave Hunter/Crown Bees)
BOTTOM: *Tiny holes in cardboard tubes indicate the presence of monodontomero, or "mono" wasps.* (Dave Hunter/Crown Bees)

completes its development inside the cocoon undetected. The wasps emerge as adults from the cocoons by chewing a tiny hole in the sides of the nesting material; they may also lay in wait until the following season. If you find unopened cocoons in late May, throw them away as a precaution. These wasps develop quickly, so multiple generations can develop each season.

What to do:

1. The most critical control method is the use of solid nesting materials free of entry points, especially at the back of the nest. Nesting materials without backs or that are too thin are easily penetrated by chalcid wasps, so be sure to use pest filters at the back of trays and cardboard tubes with inserts. Wasps rely on sonic vibrations to position their ovipositors, and it may be that this combination of barriers creates the most effective disruption.
2. Consider destroying mason bee cocoons that did not emerge by the second half of May; they may contain these parasitic wasps and should be destroyed.
3. Mono wasps are typically most active toward the end of mason bee season. Store completed nests in a BeeGuard Bag or another breathable mesh bag at the end of the nesting season. Check the bag occasionally and kill any adult wasps that may have emerged.
4. Small batches of mason bee cocoons can be hand sorted to remove chalcid wasps. You can store questionable cocoons separately in a breathable, transparent container protected from direct sunlight. Check the container often and destroy any parasitic wasps that emerge.
5. Nest materials and loose cocoons can also be protected by surrounding stored bees with

LEFT: *Ptero, or chalcid, wasp* (Dave Hunter/Crown Bees) RIGHT: *Sapygid wasp* (Eileen Krumpf/Shutterstock)

yellow sticky cards, similar to those used for house plants to trap gnats and other small insects. Only use sticky cards during mason bee storage and incubation; once the adult bees emerge, they are no longer necessary.

Pteromalus venustus (Ptero) Chalcid Wasp

Affects: leaf bees

Pteromalus, or ptero, wasps are much smaller than *Monodontomerus*, with adult females averaging 7⁄64 inch (2.5 millimeters) long. They are able to move down the nesting holes between the cocoons and the side wall. Like mono wasps, ptero wasps use their needlelike ovipositor to paralyze the bee larva by inserting it through the leafy wall. After paralyzing the bee larva, the female wasp can lay up to several dozen eggs inside the cocoon. Upon hatching, the wasp larva consumes the bee and completes its development inside the cocoon undetected. The wasps emerge as adults from the cocoons by chewing a small hole in the side. These wasps develop extraordinarily quickly, so multiple generations can develop each season, wiping out a sizable number of leaf bees in a few weeks.

What to do:

1. Keep a shop vac on hand and vacuum any of these tiny wasps that you see moving around the nesting holes. Both sexes are of a similar size, but females are black with dark brown legs and males have metallic-green heads.
2. Nest materials and loose cocoons can be protected by surrounding them with yellow sticky cards, similar to those used in house plants to trap gnats and other small insects. Only use sticky cards during leaf bee storage and incubation; once the adult bees emerge, the sticky cards are no longer necessary.

Sapygid Wasp

Affects: mason and leaf bees

While female bees are foraging away from their nests, these wasps will lay eggs in the bee nests. The developing wasp larvae consume both developing bees and their pollen loaves. These

THE LEAST CONCERNING WASP

Metallic-green native chrysidid wasps are minor predators and, luckily, often don't require control.

Female chrysidid wasps lay their eggs in nesting cavities while female mason and leaf bees are out foraging. Once the eggs hatch, the wasp larva attaches itself to the bee larva, which it begins to consume. After feeding, the wasp larva spins a thin, semitransparent cocoon and overwinters as an adult. Unlike chalcid wasps, chrysidid wasps produce only one generation per year. If you spot a large number of them hovering near your bee house, you can spray the wasps with a fine mist of water to stun them and then kill them.

Evidence of carpet beetles in damaged cocoons (Dave Hunter/Crown Bees)

wasps then spin cocoons and overwinter undetected as adults alongside neighboring bees. Watch for sapygid wasps in the summer.

What to do: If you find these parasitic wasps hovering near your bee house, spray them with a fine mist of water to stun them and then kill them.

Fruit Moth, Indian Meal Moth, Carpet Beetle, and Blister Beetle

Affects: mason and leaf bees

Moth and beetle larvae can burrow through nesting tubes and feed on pollen loaves and bee larvae. You'll notice them easily when you harvest cocoons—they are all chubby grubs of various colors and not contained within cocoons. These are attracted to the collection of bee nests in your bee house; in the wild, where nesting holes are spread widely, it's hard for the moth/beetle to easily find bee nests.

What to do: The best control method for all these species is removing and storing nesting materials after bees have completed their nesting. Store upright in a BeeGuard Bag or other breathable mesh container. When harvesting cocoons, keep an eye out and remove any fat grubs you spot.

PLANT PESTS AND THEIR BEE-SAFE REMEDIES

Reading the advertisements or package copy for garden chemicals, you can easily start thinking your yard is a war zone. Pests battle with chemicals! Diseases lurk until disaster strikes—unless additional chemical weapons are deployed! Weeds deserve life imprisonment simply because they dare to exist! At the same time, special packets of seeds promote the idea of attracting butterflies and hummingbirds—species that might be happy to visit the weeds you have been encouraged to wipe out. It is time to rethink this system.

Wherever you live, chances are you have some tricky diseases and pests that can cause real, lasting damage to your garden. The cool, damp Pacific Northwest has never met a fungus it did not embrace, and annoyingly invasive

IMPOSTER SYNDROME: CUCKOO BEES

Female cuckoo bees enter bee nests while the rightful owner is foraging and lay a single egg in the uncapped cell. Once the cuckoo bee egg hatches, the parasite larva kills its host and consumes its pollen loaf. Cuckoo bees lay only one generation per year, and their development timeline closely matches the host bee's. Since these bees tend to resemble their host bees, it is tough for nonexperts to differentiate between the pollinator and the imposter. However, there are characteristics and remedies for each species.

Mason cuckoo: slightly smaller body, no white facial hairs, no scopa

What to do: When harvesting cocoons, the cuckoo bee cocoons have a prominent nipple on one end, and you'll see long curly frass (poop). Discard any you find.

Leaf bee cuckoo: longer, more pointed abdomen with short, distinct spines at the tip

What to do: These cuckoos tend to emerge before leaf bees. Allow your bees to emerge in a BeeGuard Bag or another transparent, breathable bag, and check the early emergers to determine whether they are true leaf bees or cuckoo bees.

species like bindweed and Himalayan blackberries grow so quickly that, like the kudzu of the South, people joke about them growing right over the bodies of anyone foolhardy enough to take a midsummer nap in their backyard. The trick is knowing what genuinely needs to be dealt with, what is okay to leave alone, and what methods of control are the best choices to replace chemicals that are toxic to both people and pollinators. Think like an ecosystem! A well-balanced yard is the goal—one that combines your efforts with those of pollinators and other beneficial insects, works easily with the local climate, and naturally encourages the presence of migratory birds and butterflies. While there might be an occasional pitched battle with aphids or caterpillars or slugs, the majority of the problems are kept in check naturally. For instance, bird lovers have likely already noticed that some birds love worms and other delicious bugs far more than birdseed, so a complete absence of pests could mean fewer birds!

Some of this more natural balance is accomplished by old-fashioned physical labor. If you are dealing with rust, black spot, or powdery mildew, for example, removing the damaged leaves by hand rather than letting them fall to the ground will help interrupt the life cycle of those annoying funguses. Likewise, when you spot a major infestation of aphids, put on your gloves, grab a paper towel, and strip them off your tender plants by hand rather than running

LEFT, TOP TO BOTTOM: *The beautiful lacewing is one of the many insects essential to natural pest control. The dramatic color reversal of the twice-stabbed lady beetle gave rise to its name. The two-spotted lady beetle is common in both Europe and North America.* (Top: Christopher Bonis; middle and bottom: Jill Lightner)

for a spray. But remember that a yard with no aphids will have little food for predatory lady beetles and lacewings—and if you have a rural or suburban space large enough to make room for ground-nesting yellowjackets (see Table 1.1), they can be a real partner in managing aphid populations. Likewise, if an invasive plant species is getting out of control, go to work with a shovel, hatchet, or machete to physically knock it back rather than spraying glyphosate weed killers.

KNOW YOUR INSECTS

Insect identification is challenging for casual backyard observers—the species are seemingly endless, range from tiny to even tinier, and often have look-alike species that play a different role in the garden. Even trickier, sometimes one part of a particular insect's life cycle is harmful but another part of its life is beneficial. Helping nature maintain a balance is the key, so these micropredators and microherbivores keep each other in check with only minimal assistance from human gardeners. Almost any insect can be considered a good guy in some respects, but generally speaking, a "good guy" provides a more obvious benefit to the garden compared to a "bad guy" that may be invasive or especially persistent and difficult to manage.

Ideally, most insects, weeds, and plant diseases can manage themselves with only well-considered action from humans, and sometimes when you think through bee-friendly pest management, you realize that letting things take care of themselves is the correct path. Cleaning your bee house each season is an important action—bee houses attract too many, too varied forms of pests to skip that step. But letting a little black spot, a few aphids, and healthy patches of clover live in your garden will reduce your need for chemicals and can create a healthier habitat for all kinds of animals and plants.

Lady Beetles

Good guy, with a caveat

Lady beetles are one of the most readily identified insect species for most of us. The red or orange insects are also commonly known as ladybugs, ladybirds, and ladybird beetles, and they're adorably vicious predators—the juveniles are particularly hungry eaters of aphids,

A WORLD OF PERMACULTURE

Visiting a permaculture farm is a remarkable experience—one that might inspire you to rethink a few gardening practices or replace your last bit of lawn with a *Hügelkultur* bed or wildflower meadow. Individual farms can be found around the world, but some are open to the public only for occasional events. Others offer year-round classes, summer camp sessions, or intensive workshops devoted specifically to food production methods. And some refer to their work as "regenerative" gardening, rather than permaculture. For information, a great place to begin is Permacultureday.org, which offers a searchable map for garden tours, classes, and conferences around the world. International Permaculture Day, the first Sunday in May, has been celebrated in, so far, more than 35 countries.

The seven-spotted ladybeetle is not a North American native, but is believed to be interbreeding with native species. (Jill Lightner)

much more so than their colorful parents. Unfortunately, it's not as simple as "ladybugs are good."

Their voracious reputation, in combination with the shift of home gardeners toward natural pest control, has resulted in the rise of large-scale businesses devoted to raiding lady beetle nests in their natural environments and repackaging them for North American gardens. In this attempt at a positive change, many kinds of nonnative lady beetles have been introduced to North America from parts of Asia and Europe. The two-spotted, twice-stabbed, transverse, three-banded, and nine-spotted lady beetle species are among our native species, while the more-orange seven-spotted (one of the most common) is not. To make matters more complicated, some researchers are concerned that the seven-spotted is interbreeding with the nine-spotted. For the above reasons, it is not a good idea for gardeners to buy packaged lady beetles from garden centers as a pest control solution.

What to do: Keep aphid populations under control by combining hand harvesting (more bluntly referred to by the highly technical term "squishing") with encouraging native insect species to eat your pests. Remember that native predators and native pests evolved together over millennia, and with encouragement from your gardening practices, they will thrive together.

HOW MANY SPOTS?

While not as comprehensive as a complete field guide, you can find help in identifying your garden's lady beetles at animalspot.net/ladybugs

Syrphid Fly (Family Syrphidae)

Good guy

Also known as hoverflies, these look like honey bees, with smooth bodies and black and yellow stripes on their abdomens. They differ in a few key ways, such as having only one pair of wings (like flies) rather than two (like bees). They are also stingless, which is not necessarily a visible difference but is comforting to know as you consider how to encourage them in your garden. The nearly 900 species of North American syrphid flies can be found as adults in midsummer, feeding on pollen at many different kinds of blossoms, or around aphid colonies, where hoverflies lay their eggs. The larvae of syrphid flies are important predators of garden pests such as aphids, scales, thrips, and caterpillars; the role they play in pest control may be even more important than the adults' moderate talent for pollination. In some studies, female syrphid flies have been shown to lay more eggs in the presence of larger amounts of aphids, which is a great example of natural pest control. Some species have been estimated to eat up to 1,200 aphids each during their larval stage.

What to do:

1. If you are willing to be less vigorous when controlling aphids in spring, you may end up with many more of these hungry larvae and tiny adult pollinators as the growing season progresses.
2. Attract adult hoverflies by planting sweet alyssum, calendula, butterfly bush, borage, cosmos, asters, and Shasta daisies.

FLOAT LIKE A BUTTERFLY

As pollinators, butterflies are not nearly as efficient as bees, but the pleasure they add to the garden is undeniable. When they land on flowers, their main goal is extracting nectar, the fuel for their sometimes lengthy migrations (monarchs are unusual both in migration length and that they migrate both north and south, but other species like painted ladies, red admirals, and cloudless sulphurs also migrate seasonally). It is this migration that creates such a big difference between what they do and what bees do: While they do not pollinate much, they do visit small clusters of flowers spread over long distances, sometimes thousands of miles, while bees will visit many kinds of flowers but stick much closer to home. This gives butterflies a different role from that of either those scattershot homebodies known as mason bees or the efficient pollen-collection machines known as honey bees. Some butterfly larvae—the monarch is the most well known—have extremely specific dietary needs. If you live in a region on the monarch's migration path, or where another picky-eater species lives, plant a patch of whatever it is that they need to thrive. Monarchwatch.org can help determine which of the 73 milkweed species your region needs; garden stores that cater to your native species are also useful.

Syrphid flies (top) and painted lady butterflies (bottom) are both beneficial insects. (Bryan Reynolds)

Painted Lady Butterfly (Vanessa cardui)

Good guy

North America has more than 700 native butterfly species, and the prettier they are, the more attention they tend to get. In comparison

TOP TO BOTTOM: *Caterpillars of painted lady, mourning cloak, and variegated fritillary butterflies; welcome these in your garden!* (Top: Bryan Reynolds; middle: Michael Siluk/Shutterstock; bottom: Sari O'Neal/Shutterstock)

with the large and elegant tiger swallowtail or monarch butterflies, the smaller and more subtle painted lady receives relatively little affection. Sometimes called the thistle butterfly, the painted lady measures about 2 inches (5 centimeters) across and is primarily orange above,

Cabbage white caterpillars can do substantial damage to summer plants (Tomasz Klejdysz/Shutterstock)

with black and white wingtips and small black spots on its hind wings. Its greenish-black, somewhat bristly-looking larvae like to munch thistle (the source of its nickname), mallow, and hollyhocks, but in general it is a common, well-established, and unthreatened species that can be found from northern Mexico all the way to the southern edge of the Arctic regions.

What to do:

1. Learn to identify your region's native caterpillars and make peace with them rather than conducting search-and-destroy missions when any caterpillar dares to appear on a plant. We do not help North America's butterflies without letting caterpillars munch some leaves!
2. Plant butterfly-friendly flowers with petals that form a broad shelf to perch on while they sip nectar, like black-eyed Susans and asters.

Cabbage White Butterfly (Pieris rapae)

Bad guy

Accidentally introduced to Canada in the 1860s, today these small white butterflies—their wingspan rarely exceeds 2 inches (5 centimeters)—

are commonly found across North America. Their caterpillars are considered a serious agricultural pest, causing problems for farms raising plants in the *Brassica* genus (kale, cabbage, broccoli, and cauliflower, among others), while in their butterfly form, they do assist with the pollination of a few summertime-flowering crops. Native birds find their flavor distasteful, as these introduced caterpillars did not evolve to be part of North American native birds' diets, so it is up to you to control them if they are eating more than their fair share of your garden.

What to do: Rather than spraying—you don't want to impact leaf bees or bumble bees—check the undersides of brassica leaves and remove the small bluish-green caterpillars by hand.

Tent Caterpillars

Bad guy (least concern)

There are six species of tent caterpillar native to North America, with an additional several dozen species around the world. Tent caterpillars aren't too picky about tree species, but they are frequently drawn to fruit trees, if available. The reasons they're considered "bad" are mainly that their large, webbed nests are unsightly, and they can munch enough leaves to stress young trees. Mature trees can generally shrug off an infestation, losing a season of leaves but not taking life-threatening damage. Adult moths live for about four days and do not eat during that part of their life cycle. Bt (*Bacillus thuringiensis*) is the most common insecticide for control. While it's currently believed to have "reasonable safety to bees" compared to several other bacterial insecticides according to an analysis published by the University of Massachusetts–Amherst,[1] there's not much of a reason to use it, aside from the caterpillar "ew" factor.

What to do: Try to live with them. If you can't bring yourself to do that, or you're concerned about their impact on a young tree, use pruners to remove the nest and dispose of it without spraying.

DON'T BEE THE PROBLEM, BEE THE SOLUTION

Reducing farmers' reliance on chemical fertilizers, pesticides, and herbicides is critical for pollinators and even for the ocean. The "dead zone" in the Gulf of Mexico that is, so far, about the size of a New England state (ranging from 4,000 to almost 9,000 square miles [10,360 to 23,310 square kilometers], from 2017 to 2023) has been directly attributed to fertilizers and wastewater flowing with the Mississippi River into the Gulf. Attempts to shrink this "desert in the sea" have seen some success, but we are falling far short of the target area (1,900 square miles [4,921 square kilometers] or smaller). The use of nitrogen-heavy fertilizers has to be curtailed sharply to get closer to that goal, but the soil needs other means of getting (and remaining) healthy for that to happen.

KNOW YOUR REMEDIES

Let's say you have spotted some pests on your plants. Before grabbing any remedy at all, start by asking yourself a few somewhat philosophical questions. Remember that a large source of food attracts predators. Pests multiply quickly, but predators are slower. Wait a bit. You may find a week or two goes by and the pests are missing. Did hornets get them? Did ladybugs eat them? Allowing nature to control your yard's environment is better than our attempt at management. Why do you think the pest needs removal—is your plant being seriously damaged, or is it

YELLOWJACKETS: DESTROYER OF PICNICS, BUT NOT TRULY BAD

One insect that can cause problems for humans in the summer is the yellowjacket. Some species are native to North America, while others are recent immigrants. All can be aggressive enough to cause annoyance. In addition, they can be downright harmful to honey bee populations, by hassling and biting worker bees as they go in and out of their hive, as well as getting into the hive and eating honey and the bees themselves. (They don't tend to hassle solitary bees the same way, and they typically aren't too active during mason bee season.)

On the other hand, yellowjackets and other hornets have a natural purpose. You can find these predators patrolling raised vegetable beds, grape arbors, and other garden plants, hunting for food. In late summer, their hives swell beyond capacity, creating an environment where there is not enough natural food for them. Since late summer is the prime season to dine alfresco, it is easy to understand how our meal attracts them.

Above all, if you do run into problems with them, do not resort to sprays. Even if the spraying service or packaged product claims to be safe for children and pets, they can still harm pollinators and other beneficial insects. Remember, your garden is a complete ecosystem—one that ideally maintains a natural balance of predators and prey. While being treated as prey by yellowjackets is truly unpleasant for you and your guests at the backyard picnic table, it is not a sensible solution to wipe out every insect in the yard in a losing battle with the stripey little jerks.

What to do:

1. Provide a sacrificial plate of cut fruit and small pieces of meat about 20 feet (6 meters) from the picnic table. Set it out 20 minutes before you plan to eat, and it can serve as a magnet for hungry yellowjackets.
2. Take a paper lunch sack and mold it to look like a balloon of sorts, then hang it above where you will be eating. To a hornet it looks like a nest, and since most hornets are territorial, they tend to avoid the nest of another species.
3. Yellowjackets are typically ground nesting. Try to spot their nest and figure out what you can do to remove it entirely. If your yard is big enough and family members don't have severe allergies, you may be comfortable marking it and giving it 6 feet (1.8 meters) of space on all sides. German yellowjackets also like nesting in wood-paneled buildings, and sometimes you can find and seal the nest's entrance (or hire a professional to take care of it, making clear that you do not want to use poison).
4. Put up with it for the year and focus your efforts on trapping them early next spring. With yellowjackets, the queens are active in March, so trapping them then can have a dramatic effect on the population in the summer. They will not reuse the same nest year after year.
5. Explore homemade traps that don't impact other insects. Bait a broad, shallow bowl with water seasoned with wine or vinegar and

either dish detergent or vegetable oil. You can also add a rolled-up slice of luncheon meat pierced on a skewer; balance the skewer across the bowl. Within a few hours, the tangy vinegar scent and lure of meat may attract scores of yellowjackets, which will be trapped by the soapy or oily water.

simply less than perfect? Do you have an idea how the pest got out of control in the first place? Sometimes it is a change in the weather pattern, sometimes you simply fell behind in weeding, and sometimes it is less obvious. Last, can you think of anything you did differently last year that prevented the problem? If this questioning leads to an aha! moment, write your revelation down in a small notebook and keep it with your gardening tools as a reminder. Finally, remember to consider the option of removing a particularly needy plant entirely. Replacing it with something easier to keep healthy can offer a big sigh of relief.

Insecticidal Soap

If there was ever a mixed bag of pros and cons for a garden, it is this fatty acid–loaded type of soap. Sprayed directly on soft-bodied insects such as aphids and whiteflies, it is effective at reducing their population by as much as 65 percent. It is also approved for use on that annoying powdery mildew and can be used by certified organic farms. However, it is also known to kill a smaller percentage of beneficial insects, including ladybug larvae and lacewings, and is not particularly effective on larger pests such as caterpillars and leafhoppers. It is not known to cause much damage to bees, but it can cause unsightly damage to a wide range of plants, from tomatoes to sweet peas.

Alternatives: A mixture of 1 teaspoon (5 milliliters) of liquid dish soap to 1 quart (946 milliliters) of water is a gentler alternative, although it can still cause spots on the leaves of susceptible plants. Even safer is a hard blast of cold water, combined with hand removal of the remaining insects.

Diatomaceous Earth

Frequently suggested as a nontoxic alternative to other types of pesticides, this can damage the bodies of butterflies, some spiders, potato bugs, beetles, and even bees by creating severe dehydration. Also, beneficial hard-shelled bugs are killed by this solution. It is not recommended for a garden with healthy bees.

Alternatives: Hard-shelled insects such as ants and earwigs play beneficial roles outdoors. If your target is soft-bodied insects, try a mixture of 1 teaspoon (5 milliliters) of liquid dish soap to 1 quart (946 milliliters) of water. If your problem is slugs, try a beer trap (described below).

Slug and Snail Bait

The most common chemicals in these products are ferric phosphate and ferric sodium. The latter is particularly toxic to wildlife, and if it is sprinkled in pellet form, you cannot be sure who might eat it. Diatomaceous earth is frequently suggested for slugs, but it's not a good option for the reasons listed above.

NEONICS: THE MOST NOTORIOUS PESTICIDES

Neonicotinoids deserve some of the blame for honey bee deaths, but they are not the sole culprit. As a group, neonicotinoids are related to nicotine, which makes a certain amount of sense to anyone who has seen a 1960s-era gardening book in which a common homemade insecticide is made by soaking cigarette butts in water and then spraying the water on the affected plants. In its pure form, nicotine is a powerful neurotoxin that can easily kill humans and other large mammals. Even heavily watered down, it is capable of wiping out both good and bad garden bugs in the air, on the ground, and even underground.

Neonicotinoids hide under a variety of names at the garden center. If you spot any of these words on a package of pesticide, you have found a neonic:

- acetamiprid
- clothianidin
- dinotefuran
- imidacloprid
- nitenpyram
- thiamethoxam
- thiocloprid (also thiacloprid)

Knowing the specific names of the chemicals is much more practically useful than knowing the broad class of chemicals. No company is going to proudly proclaim they are selling you neonicotinoids anymore, but the individual chemical will be listed under active ingredients. As of 2025, eleven states have restricted residential use of this chemical class, and four states have banned all but commercial agricultural use of them, while numerous municipalities have banned or limited their use within specific cities and counties. Additionally, large chains such as Kroger, Costco, and Walmart no longer sell them. Disappointingly, Canada was prepared to ban three across the nation in 2018 but walked back those plans in 2021.

Neonicotinoids are a relatively targeted insecticide, but insecticides are only one category of the larger group called pesticides that have been designed to target funguses, bacteria, viruses, and any other kind of "pest." Pesticides as a group are worth an extra moment of your consideration. Thanks to your lovely bee haven (whether it is a current reality or a goal you are working toward), you have likely reduced your use of at least some garden toxins. However, pesticides are also present in chemicals for indoor use, including kitchen and laundry sanitizers and disinfectants, insect repellents you might use on your skin, flea and tick powders and collars, and sprays meant to kill mold or mildew in the house.

If you are steering away from these toxins outdoors, it makes sense to do the same indoors if you are able. If you go through your house removing them (it can be a time-consuming project), check your local garbage ordinances, as they often require special disposal methods.

Removing snails by hand is quicker than beer traps, and does not impact pollinators. (Jill Lightner)

Alternative: If you cannot stand removing slugs or snails by hand (washable garden gloves definitely help the "ick" factor), a few weeks' worth of beer traps might solve the problem. Set up multiple shallow containers slightly recessed into the ground and fill them about three-quarters full with beer (slugs and snails are not picky about the brand). As the critters are drawn to the smell, they will move in and get trapped. Resist the urge to clean and refill the traps frequently, as new visitors are also drawn by the scent of the snails and slugs already in the trap.

Broad-Spectrum Fungicides

These tend to be serious overkill for backyard gardeners who tire of looking at rust-spotted trees or black spot on their roses. They are known to cause issues with honey bees too, including making the bees more vulnerable to certain types of parasitic mite infestations. Even those labeled bee-safe are primarily safe for adult bees, not the larvae lying in their cocoons with a fungicide-laden pollen loaf. If you have a serious issue that truly must be treated, get the best choice you can and treat your plant when pollinators are not yet active, either at the end of the growing season or well before it starts. Check product labels carefully and try to limit your first use to one plant, in case it turns out to be problematic.

- Sulfur products: As of this writing, lime sulfur appears to be neutral for bees, but other types of sulfur-based formulas have been shown to have negative effects on honey bees (studies are only beginning in this area, but it's likely most native bees will be similarly negatively affected).
- Copper products: Liquid copper also seems to be neutral for pollinators (as far as we know as of this writing), but copper sulfate is detrimental.

Alternative: For powdery mildew and blackspot, a spray bottle filled with a mixture of one part cow's milk and two parts water has been

DANDELIONS

In many areas of North America, dandelions are one of the earliest spring flowers, and their broad, bright yellow blooms are much appreciated by our earliest bumble bee species. Consider that anything you use to treat the weeds will directly impact wild bees, so leave some dandelions for them while you dig out the rest by hand.

shown to be highly effective, particularly when sprayed preventively. If you grow roses, squash, or cucumbers, give this a try before the disease shows up and treat leaves weekly through the growing season.

Herbicides

The herbicide Roundup has been a notorious villain in organic circles for years. It contains glyphosates, which have been banned or restricted in a handful of European countries in recent years. Studies have shown their damage to pollinators, particularly honey bees and monarch butterflies at multiple stages of their respective life cycles. While less dazzling to our eyes than pollinators, earthworms and ground-dwelling insects are also harmed by glyphosates. Replacing it in your weed management gardening toolkit is key.

Alternatives:

1. Vinegar makes the pH levels in soil inhospitable to most plants, while salt turns soil into a crusty, estuary-like environment. Used together in direct application, they can be effective in killing weeds that have invaded sidewalks or patios. However, these two ingredients make soil deeply inhospitable to beneficial insects or to plants you want to grow, so use them only where you want truly barren soil.
2. Weed by hand and make peace with some of the more attractive, less invasive flowering weeds in your area.

CHAPTER 6

WILD POLLINATORS AND COMMUNITY BUILDING

I will arise and go now, and go to Innisfree,
And a small cabin build there, of clay and wattles made;
Nine bean-rows will I have there, a hive for the honey-bee,
And live alone in the bee-loud glade.

And I shall have some peace there, for peace comes dropping slow,
Dropping from the veils of the morning to where the cricket sings;
There midnight's all a glimmer, and noon a purple glow,
And evening full of the linnet's wings.

—William Butler Yeats, "The Lake Isle of Innisfree"

Yeats had the right idea back in 1888, although he was writing of an imaginary place: keeping his country's native bees, growing a tasty summer crop of fresh vegetables for himself, and finding peace in the buzzing of bees,

LEFT: *This garden center went out of its way to accommodate nesting birds.* (Jill Lightner) **RIGHT:** *A water source in the garden is useful to many species.* (Jill Lightner)

the song of crickets, and the evening's swooping around of a colorful and fairly common bird. His ideal cabin sounds a bit like a mason bee nesting hole, with its combination of clay and sticks, and a "bee-loud glade" is something every gardener might aspire to create.

In a bee-friendly garden ecosystem, there are plenty of warm, sweet fragrances for you to enjoy from your favorite chair. With a natural balance of tiny predators and prey, it functions easily on its own without you spending your days and evenings fussing with unhealthy plants. A garden is not meant to be only chores but for your enjoyment—and once it has been designed to work with your climate and native critters, you will have more time to put your feet up and enjoy a beverage while the pollinators flit around you in the "purple glow" of noon. This is the blissful, lazy summer that Yeats was dreaming of in his poem, and it is still the subject of pop songs today.

Chances are you know someone with such a serious fear of bees, the idea of a bee-filled garden is enough to send them screeching inside with a panicked look in their eyes. It is a common enough fear that there are two official names for it: melissophobia and apiphobia (they mean essentially the same thing, and oddly enough, both words literally refer to a fear of honey bees). Sadly, it is almost always the more territorial, aggressive yellowjackets that are responsible for the fear, and your average acquaintance cannot tell the difference between the yellowjacket who stung them badly at a picnic and the mellow, vegetarian bees collecting pollen. However, honey bees do not help allay this fear. They do indeed sting (as we all know from those protective spacesuits that beekeepers wear), and if we spot a swarm, it is downright intimidating—we know those little worker bees are armed and ready in defense mode as they protect their queen on the move.

It is true that nobody enjoys being stung, but official estimates are that only about 3 percent of adults are seriously allergic. The total number of sting-related deaths in the United States each year is around 40, which is not too different from the country's annual number of deaths from lightning. Some phobia cases are so severe that even gentle mason and leaf bees are terrifying, but if you patiently encourage a friend to join you in your garden for a visit, they might discover that the majority of bees have far more interest in pollen and nectar than they do in humans. After all, stings typically occur when someone threatens (or accidentally threatens) the hive. Avoid getting one caught in your sleeve or trapped in your soda can, and it's not hard to share your outdoor space with a variety of bees and wasps.

BEE AMBASSADOR: PUBLIC RELATIONS BEGINS WITH YELLOWJACKETS

Yellowjacket behavior is probably the number one reason that people fear all bees, as they don't understand the behavioral differences between territorial, queen-defending hornets and yellowjackets and the mild-mannered, solitary leaf and mason bees. Midsummer is the time of year when everyone heads outside, and nurseries and garden centers are packed on weekends as people tweak their garden design or work on full-scale landscaping projects.

All this outdoor activity makes it a great time to take the spotlight off of yellowjackets with

LEFT: *Don't let a fear of yellowjackets blind you to the tremendous benefits of a bee-friendly garden.* (Christopher Bonis) **RIGHT:** *Summer bees and beneficial wasps overwinter as larvae.* (Dave Hunter/Crown Bees)

Show your successful bee houses to friends and neighbors and encourage them to add one to their garden as well. (Dave Hunter/Crown Bees)

a little public relations work. This is an easy opportunity to act as a "bee ambassador"—whether you post images of your bee house on social media, explain why you introduced them to your garden over lunch with friends, or sign up for more official programs, like giving a neighborhood garden tour or offering to speak to a local garden club. While honey bee–centered classes will always draw curious gardeners, a talk on the simplicity of gentle bees may be welcome too.

Many people (including dedicated organic gardeners) have either never heard of mason and leaf bees or once tried to set some up with a drilled block of wood and failed, not understanding the issues that arise from that style of nesting box (see chapter 2). Most of the time, when you tell people about the amazing solitary bee that rarely stings, they will immediately see the sense in introducing them to the garden. You can show off your setup, explain how easy it is, and either connect them with where you purchased your setup or offer DIY tips. You can promise a gift of extra cocoons when the season is right the following year.

If your friends tried the drilled block of wood at some point in the past, you will likely be told a story along the lines of "I used to keep them, but one year they didn't hatch so I took the block down. Mason bees don't work for me." When you explain that the block likely got infested by parasites or mold, it is an easy point in their education to show your individual tubes or trays and emphasize how your small extra efforts in bee husbandry pay off by keeping disease and predators at bay, while not requiring more than a few hours of your time each year. Avoid accidentally shaming them, though—nobody wants to feel harshly judged over something they didn't know.

Your demonstrations and expertise will be particularly compelling if you can time them to show off an abundant crop of cherries, apricots, or apples, while providing a comparison with what your harvest was before adding bees. "Before and after" photos, showing what your trees or bushes looked like before you introduced these friendly pollinators to your garden and then after, are another great way to illustrate the dramatic increase in fruit that is possible once you create a bee haven and have a successful year of solitary bees.

NORTH AMERICAN NATIVE SPECIES

Each region has its own types of native pollinators. Many species are members of a broad family that share similar traits and preferences, although some of the specific details may vary across the continent.

Something you will discover quickly is that having one kind of pollinator in your garden "bee-gets" another. That is great news for the ecosystem you have been stewarding, because different pollinators tend to prefer different plants and fulfill a variety of roles by simply being themselves. Some birds and insects get a bit more credit for pollinating than they truly deserve, while others do not get nearly enough. In most cases, it is easy to spot them and tell them apart, but it is useful to know what they are all doing.

The simplest method of attracting native pollinators is to plant gardens primarily made up of native wildflowers, grasses, shrubs, and trees. The Natural Resources Conservation Service at the USDA suggests a goal of at least 75 percent native species for a truly sustainable native wildlife habitat, but for urban environments, this high of a percentage may be a struggle. Native plants are adapted to your local climate and soils and have evolved hand in hand with your region's native pollinators, but they may not be made to withstand modern problems like car exhaust, overhead electric wires, or a lack of mature native trees providing shade canopy.

Perhaps you cannot single-handedly bring back black bears or beavers to your city garden or suburban yard, but a generous variety of native wildflowers and grasses will provide your local pollinators with edible nectar and pollen and leaves for their larvae, while shrubs and trees provide important shelter, nesting material, and winter habitat. When you are selecting nonnative plants for your garden, consider the following points for both plant variety and

DOGS AND BEES

Have a dog who loves to snap at bees? You are not alone: Numerous dogs get into the habit of snapping at anything that buzzes near them, while others seem to zero in on a single species of insect. There is no specific reason for it, other than that dogs like to chase things and catch them in their mouths. But while having your dog remove houseflies is kind of a handy trick, it is best to discourage it from snapping at and eating bees. We know pollinators are in trouble, and having dogs take out our nearby bees is no different from having an outdoor housecat kill songbirds. Additionally, some dogs have serious, painful reactions to bee stings if they catch a bumble bee, honey bee, or wasp. To avoid vet bills, and help keep pollinator populations healthy, teach your dog to "leave it" with bees, as you would if they were eating your shoes.

LEFT: *Bumble bees are particularly attracted to all types of alliums.* (Jill Lightner) **RIGHT:** *Bees, such as this bumble bee, are particularly attracted to purple flowers.* (Jill Lightner)

garden design to make a positive impact for native pollinators.

First, choose perennials instead of annuals. Perennials provide a dependable food source year after year, plus they are generally richer in nectar. Try to keep your blossom shapes pollinator friendly—hybridized "double" flowers such as marigolds, fuchsias, hollyhocks, petunias, and roses have been bred to appeal to humans, not easy pollen and nectar access.

Second, grow each species of flower in a clump or cluster of a single variety, as a landscape like this will attract more pollinators than individual plants all mixed together. Birds and butterflies tend to favor bell-, tube-, or trumpet-shaped flowers, especially when rimmed with a flat surface for perching. Broadly, bees are most attracted to fragrant purple, blue, and yellow flowers (they cannot see the color red), while night-blooming flowers (usually white and strongly scented) support moths. Butterflies and hummingbirds can both see the color red and seem to like it and other rich, bright colors; hummingbirds are perfectly content with unscented flowers.

Third, provide water, both as a tool for survival and a simple attractant. A source of water such as a birdbath, fountain, or pond with flat rocks for landing will attract some wasps, bumble bees, honey bees, butterflies, and hummingbirds. White, crimson, and red clovers, which are members of the legume family that includes beans and peanuts, provide abundant nectar and tender leaves.

Finally, grow a variety of foliage plants, which provide necessary food for pollinator larvae in addition to bird nesting material. Planting a dense hedge of a single type of evergreen is easy for you, but not ideal for anything else.

BUMBLE BEES (GENUS *BOMBUS*)

There are 46 species of bumble bee native to North America, and while they have a few visible differences, they also have much in common. All are fat and furry to a degree; some have a nearly uniform color (black or orange-gold) while other species have one or more stripes. They do not dig or tunnel, but they will make use of existing burrows (like abandoned rodent dens) and live in small colonies of up to 400. Bumble bees are far less aggressive than yellowjackets but may sting if they feel that their home or queen is threatened. While they do not "waggle dance" like honey bees, they communicate with each other by pheromones and pollen exchanges, which lets their hive mates know when a good source of food has been found. Like honey bees, and unlike mason and leaf bees, they are dedicated to transporting larger amounts of pollen and nectar back to their hives via pollen baskets; this makes them good pollen collectors and less effective pollinators. Many bumble bees have special relationships with one type of flower (referred to as "constancy"), so they can be more useful as pollinators of single-species agricultural fields.

Frighteningly enough, wild bee populations are struggling. Seven yellow-faced Hawaiian bees, as well as Oregon's Franklin's bumble bee and the rusty patch bumble bee of the upper Midwest and eastern Canada, are listed as endangered species in the United States as of 2024. Additional species are experiencing dramatic loss, and petitions have been submitted for three of them to be considered for the endangered species list. The problems they face are not the same as CCD. It appears that a mix of pesticide and herbicide use, chemically treated agricultural seed, problems from imported fungus, and serious habitat loss have added up to disaster fairly quickly.

However, some slightly encouraging signs have been reported in recent years. In 2013, a community scientist named Will Peterman chased down a year-old rumor and found a

PLAYTIME FOR BUMBLE BEES

In 2022, researchers at Queen Mary University of London were studying how lab bumble bees learned behavior from each others and noticed that some of them seemed to move small wooden balls around for no clear reason. When the lab nesting boxes were rearranged to create "rec rooms" where bumble bees could go a bit out of their way to roll these balls, many did so, particularly young bees (similar to how young mammals are more likely to play than adults). It is possible that bee brains benefit from play in childhood like other species do. Experiments are ongoing, and if nothing else, researchers believe that knowing bumble bees are capable of play behavior helps humans feel more empathy for them, and perhaps more protective of them in the wild.

Orange belted bumble bees are one of the 46 species of bumble bees native to North America. (Bill Rogers)

small colony of western bumble bees (*Bombus occidentalis*) in a park north of Seattle. This bee had not been seen in the Puget Sound area since the 1990s. His find spurred other people to speak up about bees they had seen (the species has an easily noticeable white rump), and Peterman and some volunteers were able to confirm living colonies in four areas around Seattle.

A crowdfunding campaign netted enough money for Peterman's volunteer group to fund a data- and sample-collecting trip through eight regions, stretching from Washington to New Mexico. A hopeful discovery is that the western bumble bee has perhaps begun to adapt to the microsporidian parasite *Nosema bombi*, which is closely related to the forms of nosema that are causing such trouble for honey bees. While this is a specific example of a potentially rebounding bee that had been in trouble, bumble bees as a whole are still at a point where the choices we make in our gardens can help them out.

If you want to learn more about bumble bees, including how to identify them based on the region where you found them and their pattern of stripes, start with your state's or province's fish and game or wildlife agency website; they can be terrific sources for identification photos, conservation status reports, and community science projects—depending on the health of local populations, there may be a true need to identify and report specific bumble bee sightings.

Bumble bees love lavender, salvia, beebalm, flowering thyme, artichoke flowers, and alliums of all sizes, from chives to the baseball-size white puffball flowers that appear if you plant the roots attached to the scallions you bought at the grocery store. Save a few inches of the white tips (with roots attached) and plant them in your vegetable garden, watering regularly, until you see new life sprouting from their tops. Not only will you have an endless crop of green onions, but bumble bees seem to adore the blooms.

Building a Bumble Bee Box

Bumble bees are generally able to find a cozy, dry cavity in the ground where a queen can begin her nest, but creating a nesting box is easy. Because they are social bees, there is no need for individual nesting tubes. The Xerces Society recommends enough preservative-free lumber to make a box in the neighborhood of 7 inches (18 centimeters) square. It is important that all corners and seams be weathertight, as mold or fungus will grow if water gets in, and larvae need to stay warm and snug, well protected from drafts. Drill a few small holes in the top and bottom for drainage and ventilation, and cover them with mesh. A short length of ¾-inch (2-centimeter) plastic pipe is the right size to insert in a hole in the front for an entrance. Tuck in a generous amount of fluffy, natural bedding material, like the unbleached cotton batting sold for quilting or upholstery projects.

Once it is built, the box should rest on the ground or be buried, with the entrance hole well exposed and set at a slight slope. Make sure to place it in a shady, out-of-the-way spot where it will not be disturbed and will not get flooded in heavy rainfall. Set your new box out in spring when you spot your first bumble bee; if it does not have any inhabitants by mid-July, go ahead and put it in storage until the following spring. Once a bumble bee box has been used, it will never be used again. When you open it up in the fall, you'll be amazed at the mess your visiting pollinators left behind. Replace the box with a new one the following spring!

Climate Change and Ground-Nesting Bees

As the effects of climate change have become more widespread, an increasing amount of data has shown that ground-nesting bees will particularly feel its impacts. Bumble bees, with their large, furry bodies, are better adapted to cooler temperatures, but North America (and the rest of the world) is trending warmer and seeing longer, hotter heat waves. This heat also wrecks wildflowers that bees would normally seek out for their nectar and pollen. The US Fish and Wildlife Service was conducting studies in 2024 to learn what they can from bumble bees in Colorado and Oregon, especially their overwintering habits and heat stress. While there is much to learn—as quickly as possible—university and government researchers agree that providing native wildflowers and habitat suitable for ground-nesting bees is key for now. In 2023, the US Department of Energy reminded anyone who sets up a bee house or nesting box that welcomes any species to clean it annually to avoid spreading disease.

CONNECTING COMMUNITIES AND POLLINATOR ACTIVISM

Pollinators have no respect for borders. Therefore, the most successful support efforts for them tend to work at a large scale and cover all aspects of the environments that bees, bats, wasps, and butterflies need to thrive. Depending on your particular region or interest, these organizations are a great place to learn about recent scientific breakthroughs and upcoming community science projects or grant opportunities.

Pollinator Partnership

The Pollinator Partnership is the world's largest organization dedicated to the protection of pollinators and their ecosystems. Its North American Pollinator Protection Campaign is a collaboration that brings together 170 organizations, institutions, and businesses, from the US Department of the Interior to universities throughout Canada, the United States, and Mexico to five separate seed companies (see Resources).

The campaign was launched in 1999 and has carried out a number of large-scale projects that add up to remarkable progress, including the signing of 11 pollinator-protection agreements with the federal agencies responsible for the management of over 1.5 billion acres (607 million hectares) of land. It is the sort of work that tends to be entirely behind the scenes for most US residents but can add up to incredibly important policies governing federal land. More readily apparent projects include the sponsorship of Pollinator Week (with events and media coverage at both the state and federal level) and the development of well-targeted planting guides that serve as a fantastic resource for every part of the United States and two regions in Canada (see Resources).

Pollinator Week occurs in most states annually in mid-June (the precise dates shift a bit each year, but the dates for the next one can be found at Pollinator.org, along with an event map). Across the country, this is the week to find pollinator garden–themed events, from a pollinator-centered "Swamp Tromp" at the Karen T. Marcus Sandhill Crane Access Park near West Palm Beach, Florida, to a Spanish-language presentation titled "Polinizadores en su Jardín" at the Latino Center of the Midlands in Omaha, Nebraska. If you are a member of a garden club, volunteer for your farmers market, or are involved with a local apiary club, Pollinator Week is a great time to host a solitary bee–themed event, whether your group is trying to grow your community of mason beekeepers or wants to show how productive leaf bees are as they buzz about your garden during their prime season of activity. It is the most common time of year to see parks, libraries, and garden centers host speakers on the topic of pollination.

The Great Sunflower Project

The Great Sunflower Project (greatsunflower .org) was launched in 2008 by a small group

CREATING A SALT LICK

Many kinds of butterflies and bees appreciate a damp salt lick, and the process of creating one is not that different from what you did for your mason bees' mud patch. Start with an area fairly free of vegetation and moisten the ground with a dripping hose or drip irrigation line. Once it is nice and damp, mix a small amount of noniodized sea salt or wood ashes into the mud. Salt licks provide key minerals for some species of pollinators, but remember that salt is an exceptional herbicide. If you are going to create a salt lick, choose a site where you do not want living plants.

Native flowers in large clumps are easier for bees to find than sparse plantings. (Jill Lightner)

at the University of California–Santa Barbara headed by Gretchen LeBuhn, and it's still going strong as of 2024. This project has two goals: first, to determine where pollinator populations are declining, and second, to improve pollinator habitat.

When LeBuhn realized that nobody had ever measured the amount of pollination happening across a region (the project's goal is the entire North American continent), she and her team set out to look at how a decline in bee populations can influence our gardens. Planting the specific sunflower varietal Lemon Queen aids in the collection of a specific set of data, as part of the Safe Gardens for Pollinators program. Separately, the

POLLINATOR FIGHT CLUB

In December 2022, Thomas Renaud and Meredith Root-Bernstein published a paper documenting something you may have witnessed: pollinator fights—mostly dive-bombing but also kicking—on flowers when multiple species are trying to collect pollen.[1] During 48 hours of observation across parks in Paris, the research team noted that aggressive behavior didn't begin with the bees that humans associate with hive-defending behavior. While the specific species will vary depending on where you live, expect that honey bees and bumble bees (along with butterflies) will be the least aggressive brawlers at the pollen bar, while carpenter bees and hoverflies are the most likely to start fights.

Pollinator Friendly Plants program is designed to identify key plant varietals that best support healthy pollinator communities.

Both of these programs are designed to be easy to participate in. Start by registering for an online account. Then, either grow some Lemon Queen sunflowers or find a single plant in your yard that you can identify with certainty, such as a Gravenstein apple tree, bachelor's button, or Spanish lavender. Sit and observe your chosen plant for at least five minutes, recording each and every pollinator that visits. Make sure you look at only one plant, and not a row or collection of them if, say, you have a lavender hedge! Finally, log in to your Great Sunflower account and record your data. You can record as many observations as you want while your flowers are in bloom; it is up to you whether that is once a year or a weekly effort during the entire blooming season.

You can make an interesting comparison by choosing two different kinds of plants, both blooming in the same season, and observe one while a friend or family member observes the other. This can quickly reveal which of your plants your pollinators are most drawn to, which is useful both to your own garden design and to the data collection project, helping it identify not only which plants pollinators love, but which ones they tend to not visit as regularly. The online form notes that if you saw no pollinators at all, you should be sure to mark that box: Total absence is one of the most important data points they can receive.

If you take the opportunity, you will also likely discover that one bee species is particularly drawn to one type of plant, while a different bee species noticeably prefers another. One observer in the Northwest found that while bumble bees were all over his raspberry canes, mason bees ignored the raspberries and showed a strong preference for the marionberry canes a few feet away. To a human, the blooms are essentially the same, but for bees they are clearly different, and clearly the bees have their preferences! That said, if there is only one flower available to generalists, they will pollinate it. What can you observe and report from your own bee haven?

The island marble butterfly is a pollinator success story. (U.S. Fish & Wildlife Service, CC BY 2.0/Wikimedia Commons)

Spineless Is Beautiful

The Xerces Society might be familiar to you already; it has been working to protect invertebrates and their wide variety of habitats since 1971, and while it is cited frequently in reports about pollinators, its work extends to encompass critical species such as sea stars, freshwater shellfish, earthworms, and the humble sea sponge. Because these varied species play key (and often unsung) roles in ecosystems around the world, their success is the basis for the survival of everything from the stunning coral reefs of Belize to the alpine meadows of the Rockies.

In addition to helping fund academic research on pollinators, aquatic species, and endangered animals, the society leads substantial efforts to reduce the impact of pesticides, particularly in wetlands and on farms, and has developed a handful of inspiring community science projects. From a one-day count of western monarch butterflies on their migration to a more complex project on migrating dragonflies, the Xerces Society (at xerces.org) is a terrific resource for those looking for both recent academic research and family-friendly science projects. Its name, in honor of the first known North American butterfly to go extinct, is a constant reminder of why its work, along with all of our own pollinator-centric efforts, is critical.

They've been fighting on behalf of another butterfly, the island marble, for more than two decades. This small green-and-white pollinator was believed extinct in the United States back in 1908, but one last population was identified on San Juan Island in 1998. The Xerces Society was one of several groups to first petition for its protection as an endangered species in 2002; it finally earned that status in 2020. This means that funding is available to protect its habitat at American Camp at San Juan Island National Historical Park and educate island landowners on what these small butterflies need to survive. From planting specific types of flowering mustard plants to learning how to identify and protect the eggs and caterpillars (browsing deer contribute to the butterfly's decline) to shifting garden care away from mowing and pesticide use, the efforts to support the island marble are an example of how the protection of one species can encourage actions that protect many species.

EVOLVING SCIENCE AND POLLINATORS

Like all good science, entomology is continually evolving. As researchers race to solve the large-scale problems of CCD, out-of-control parasites, and rapidly falling populations of wild bees, new hypotheses are being developed and tested continually. Much has been learned in recent years, ranging from what species of parasites and types of viruses seem to be causing the worst troubles to the health effects of pesticides, herbicides, and habitat loss.

When it comes to habitat loss, people tend to focus on the more obvious species: Many programs in the Pacific Northwest, for instance, are devoted to habitat restoration for the region's native salmon runs. From urban watershed restoration and dam removals to the Salmon-Safe certification of large suburban corporate headquarters to farm-based projects that encourage farmers to leave wild buffers around rivers and streams, these programs are all targeted at a small handful of species (a few kinds of wild salmon and trout) but can result in important changes for related populations, such as migratory birds, small mammals, and freshwater shellfish.

Monarchs

There are also projects emphasizing pollinator habitat, in large part because of the troubled monarch butterfly. Migrating thousands of miles each year, the gorgeous monarch needs not only nectar-producing plants for itself but also milkweed plants for its larvae to feed upon; they also require water and sizable trees for roosting. They are so widespread that they are the official state insect for seven states, covering an enormous section of the United States, from Vermont to Idaho and from Minnesota to Texas.

In 2014, the Center for Biological Diversity joined with the Center for Food Safety to propose protecting monarch butterflies under the Endangered Species Act because their population had fallen off dramatically both east and west of the Rockies—up to 90 percent of the eastern population seemed to have vanished. Monarchwatch.org, a program founded at the University of Kansas in 1992, includes a variety of projects, such as spreading milkweed seeds throughout the butterflies' migration routes. With the larvae dependent on milkweed for food, this one family of plants is key to saving this beautiful species. Large-scale habitat restoration projects in the right regions can apply for free milkweed pods to plant.

The Tribal Environmental Action for Monarchs, or TEAM coalition, was begun in 2015 as one of the first examples of intertribal environmental collaborations. Based in Oklahoma, it has brought together seven Native American tribes to help protect and restore the monarch: Chickasaw, Citizen Potawatomi, Eastern Shawnee, Miami Nations, Muscogee Creek, Osage, and Seminole. Together, they have restored over 60,000 milkweeds and 40,000 native wildflowers to date on 2,250 acres (910 hectares) of land.

Monarchs east of the Rockies are also getting straightforward funding assistance for habitat restoration. Georgia hosts Monarchs Across Georgia, providing grants particularly for milkweed planting, while the Iowa Department of Natural Resources is working to protect and expand natural prairie wildflowers that provide crucial pollen for the butterflies in addition to milkweed for their larvae to munch. While monarch butterflies are the focal species of all these

A beautiful pollinator, the monarch butterfly needs milkweed to survive. (Christopher Bonis)

WENDY CALDWELL

EXECUTIVE DIRECTOR, MONARCH JOINT VENTURE

The name seems vague, but in the realm of conservation, a joint venture describes a specific type of partnership that connects government agencies, tribes, nonprofits, corporations, and individuals to implement a plan within a geographical area. In some cases, that area can be an entire continent, but however large the area, the ideal result is deep collaboration and shared perspectives as all work toward a common goal. The Monarch Joint Venture (MJV) works in Mexico, the United States, and Canada to protect the migration of the monarch butterfly. Wendy Caldwell began working with them in 2013 and became their executive director in 2018. Since 2008, the MJV has put science into action through the Monarch Conservation Implementation Plan.

Monarch migration occurs across many habitats and of course ignores state, provincial, and national borders, making international collaboration an absolute necessity. In an email, Caldwell explained, "Our key focus is finding innovative ways to engage people and organizations in monarch conservation and to use that as a way to contribute to broader conservation and sustainability efforts. We have four pillars of work: habitat conservation, science, education, and partnership."

From online educational efforts that help gardeners identify, find, and successfully grow the correct variety of milkweed for their area to habitat-mapping projects on US Bureau of Land Management lands, the MJV takes a science-driven, interdisciplinary approach to their programs. They also provide grants to a lengthy list of partners, including Crown Bees, the Xerces Society, Pollinator Partnership, Cibolo Nature Center, the University of Wisconsin Arboretum, and the Iowa Department of Natural Resources. Their website (monarchjointventure.org) is a useful source for monarch-focused community science projects from northern Mexico to Canada and from rural desert habitats to urban parks.

Each month they host a free webinar that covers an enormous variety of topics, like improving science education in preschool, container gardening to support native biodiversity, large-scale solar project design, USDA climate initiatives, and basic monarch biology. You never know where a simple webinar for a casually interested viewer may lead. Caldwell wrote, "The people-power required for coordinating, advocating for, studying, teaching about, and implementing conservation action is often underestimated, or undervalued. The people that dedicate their lives to this work navigate many challenges, work to build new and strengthen key relationships, and are always finding ways to innovate and find new solutions, often on a shoestring budget. People are what drives this mission forward, and we all have a role to play." Caldwell's interest in monarchs is rooted in her childhood 4H club and an insect collection she exhibited at fairs in her home state—her career can inspire any parent or educator who tries to spark interest in kids. Caldwell offers this astonishing fact to pass along: "A monarch caterpillar grows 2000 times its original mass just by eating milkweed over about two weeks, which is about the equivalent of a human baby growing to the size of an elephant."

Caldwell emphasizes that a key role for those along the monarch migration path is to grow milkweed (see Resources) and provide pollinator-friendly habitats; unlike some pollinators, monarchs can be effectively supported by a patchwork of home gardens. Wherever you live, it pays to know your caterpillars. Caldwell applauds both the iNaturalist app and the Peterson and Princeton field guides to caterpillars.

efforts, what helps the habitat of one pollinator improves the habitat for all of them.

Hummingbirds

The long, narrow beaks of hummingbirds are specifically adapted so that the birds can drink nectar from tubular-shaped blossoms, which they incidentally help pollinate while they are feeding. East of the Mississippi River, the ruby-throated hummingbird (*Archilochus colubris*) is the sole breeding species, while all along the Pacific coast and stretching into the Southwest, the spunky Anna's hummingbird (*Calypte anna*) is common in urban areas. There are several other hummingbirds throughout North America too, with the number of species increasing in the southwestern United States and throughout Mexico and the Caribbean. They are all terrific little pest controllers, continually picking off aphids, small caterpillars, and insect eggs along with sipping nectar. All species are migratory, but in places with mild winters, such as the Pacific Northwest or the mid-Atlantic coast, they will happily stick around all year if well-stocked feeders are available.

Make sure you use plain sugar to mix their food (a ratio of four parts water to one part sugar does the trick), not honey or artificial sweeteners, and scrub that feeder at least weekly, as it can grow mold that will quickly kill hummingbirds. There is no good reason that commercial feeder mixes use artificial red dyes, so if you make your own, do not bother adding food coloring to your mix.

While there is a widespread belief that hummingbirds particularly love red and purple flowers, and their eyes are able to see them, feeder-visiting species do not tend to be picky and are as perfectly content to drink nectar from pale yellow honeysuckle as they are from more

Hummingbirds not only are excellent pollinators, they help control garden pests too. (Robert Brown/iStock)

colorful trumpet vines. More elusive varieties like the extra-teeny calliope (*Selasphorus calliope*) or brightly colored rufous (*Selasphorus rufus*) are most appreciative of regional wildflowers. As they both have remarkably widespread territories—particularly given their small size—it is best to seek out wildflower seed packets appropriate for your area and plant accordingly. As with all pollinators, if you plant it, they will come.

Bats

Bats are evening pollinators (and hungry predators of many annoying insects) that have been suffering from a completely different issue: A fungal disease known as white-nose syndrome was first identified in New York in 2007. It has since spread to all but a few states and eight out of ten Canadian provinces, killing millions of bats across the continent and doing particular harm to three bat species formerly common across New England.

Progress has been made against this infection, thanks to a team of three researchers: USDA Forest Service scientists Sybill Amelon and Dan Lindner, and Chris Cornelison of Georgia State University. They grew a common North American bacterium in a different place from where it usually grows—on the mineral cobalt. This resulted in a cure that works in remarkably low doses and is easy to distribute through sick bat populations, thanks to the way this new compound flows through the air into the bats' hibernation caves (which is where the fungus is spread). Trials of this vaccine are showing it to be of use, and studies are ongoing in multiple states as of the 2023–2024 bat hibernation season.

Getting healthy bat populations back in action means fewer farmers and backyard gardeners will feel driven to resort to chemical pesticides—chemicals that are likely to cause only greater harm to other species if used. It is a clear example of how the health of one animal affects the health of all the rest. According to the US Geological Survey, whose work includes biology, in "the United States alone, bats are estimated to save farmers at least $3.7 billion per year in pest control services."[2] If bats are not fulfilling their role of eating insects, then humans will not simply adjust to living with that many more insects—instead, we will go straight for the chemical solution. Better to cure the bats and restore their population as much as possible.

If you have noticed bats where you live (even in cities, they are a fairly common sight near lakes at dusk), or you would like to learn more about why you are not finding them in your area, there are a few organizations dedicated to building bat houses and hosting evening bat walks and other interesting events. There are seasonal "bat cams" that let you watch what bats get up to inside their homes. Visit Batcon.org for a broad spectrum of information with a North American focus or Batworld.org for a global organization that includes rehabilitation and sanctuary among its efforts.

BATS IN YOUR ATTIC

Little brown bats are found in forest habitats in Canada and Alaska throughout the continental United States and into central Mexico. When they share an area with humans, they are greatly appreciative of a snug northern attic to roost in over the summer and raise their young, before heading farther south to hibernate. While nesting bats aren't the easiest housemates for odor reasons, they won't destroy wiring and insulation like mice do. If you evict a group from your home when they are raising their young, chances are you've wiped out that group forever. As with yellowjackets, it's best that you put up with their presence for the season, until the young are grown and gone, and then clean up your attic and seal it against their future use.

CHAPTER 7

SAVING OUR FOOD SUPPLY, ONE GARDEN AT A TIME

Ideally, food should be a way of joyfully connecting with each other, both to our immediate neighbors and to cultures around the world, through laughter, shared effort, generosity, and love. Too often, we're faced with local or global scarcity due to climate change and transportation problems, increasing expenses, nutrition concerns, and health fears, all of which lead to divisive emotions. It was not meant to be like this. The way forward is to collaborate at all levels, across many fields of expertise, sprinkling education and affection across communities like a gentle dusting of pollen.

For good or ill, North America continues to urbanize. Statistics Canada/Statistique Canada shared this summary in 2022: "With population growth rates reaching up to 10.6%, 18 of the 25 largest municipalities grew at a faster pace than Canada overall (5.2%) from 2016 to 2021."[1] In the same period, urban growth in the United States continued, with the biggest new

Raised gardens are attractive and can provide great pollen for bees and food for humans. (Courtesy of Seattle Department of Neighborhoods P-Patch Program)

growth areas shifting south to metro areas in Florida, Texas, and Arizona.[2] Meanwhile, US farmland trends in the 21st century are well established and shown in each farm census: a loss of total acreage; a consolidation of land ownership leading to fewer, larger farms; and striking growth in the cost of chemicals each farm purchases.[3] While the number of acres with commercial orchards has grown, it hasn't been nearly enough to offset the decrease in acres devoted to almost every crop. To shift food more thoroughly into a force for good—abundant health, cooperative communities, thriving local economies, and affordable quality—it is important that urban diners find ways to connect with the food supply, reduce food waste, and support their most local agriculture.

FOOD, FARMS, AND GARDENS

While denser communities can have positive benefits relating to efficient use of resources and infrastructure spending, until recently city dwellers tended to be disconnected from where their food originates, unless they shop directly at farmers markets or are customers of a farm-direct CSA (community-supported agriculture) program. People who do shop for some or all of their food through these options help farmers take back at least some control over their own production, as they remove mandates dictated by packing houses, wholesale buyers, and other food processors. It takes a little more effort on both sides to create direct connections between small, rural farmers and urban or suburban households.

One cheerful shift in this disconnect comes from the US-based National Gardening Association, whose data shows both an increase in edible gardens and a reduction in lawn care expenditures every year since 2019.[4] This growth is across all income levels and all age groups and includes both city and suburban residents. Still,

Planting clumps of flowers in vegetable beds can attract pollinators, which in turn can boost harvest. (Gina Lee Rodgers/Shutterstock)

the vast majority of food originates on farms. Even dedicated home gardeners who raise a few poultry for eggs will still buy items that either cannot be grown locally (like bananas and pineapples), need a fair amount of land to grow in family-sized amounts (rice or wheat), or require processing before we eat them (olive and canola oils). While you have learned how mason and leaf bees can pollinate in your own garden, the larger workings of a farm are more mysterious.

POLYCULTURE AND REGENERATIVE AGRICULTURE

The idea of balance in nature applies equally to a balanced yard or a balanced farm, and *polyculture* is the term used when gardeners or farmers apply the concept of nature's diversity to their own well-tended plots. A classic bee haven uses many polyculture techniques, such as companion planting, intercropping (planting many species of plant rather than one across a large section of land), and maintaining beneficial weeds. The polyculture concept also applies to ranchers, who might raise a mixture of chickens, turkeys, hogs, sheep or goats, and cattle on a much smaller acreage than the typical single-species ranch, making use of clever pasture-rotation systems. However it is applied, it simply means many diverse species growing together.

Regenerative agriculture is a "yes, and" addition to polyculture. Its broad-ranging goals include striving for equity, increasing climate resiliency, and improving the health of ecosystems by using principles that are often rooted in land management practices of Indigenous communities like intensive rotational grazing and agroforestry. These techniques are not always relevant to home gardeners with a small raised bed or two, but many can be scaled down, lightly adapted, or brought to your urban community garden.

This all relates to our desire for more bee havens abuzz with mason and leaf bees alongside healthy honey bee hives and bumble bee nests. As there is no one plant we should grow to feed the world, there is no single pollinator that can do all the work we need. Each pollinator has its prime season, its preferred plants, its unique needs, its ideal setting, and its own quirky personality. If you can create a garden that supports healthy populations of several species, you are doing more than your own garden a favor; you are setting an example that the rest of your community can emulate once they understand why it matters.

The word *permaculture* was coined in 1978 by two Australians: Bill Mollison and David Holmgren. In a nutshell, it is about working with nature rather than battling it. If you have ever been lucky enough to stand in the midst of an old-growth forest, you have seen deep layers of plants and animals working together, with nothing going to waste and a remarkable diversity of life being maintained, from tiny leafcutter ants and fungus the size of a coffee table to towering trees and the birds that live only in their uppermost branches. These forests evolved over thousands of years and still function as a whole—and it is sadly easy for modern civilization to eradicate one part of the whole, doing tremendous damage. When people think of permaculture in relation to their yards, it's likely not about creating a straight-up duplication of the wild environment but about looking at the yard as a whole ecosystem, with the climate and soil health as fundamental pieces of the whole. Paul Wheaton of Permies.com describes permaculture as "having a more symbiotic relationship with nature, so I can be even lazier." The result, ideally, is bountiful crops laid out in a natural pattern rather than in uniform rows requiring excess attention, water, and resources. Once a yard or farm is designed to flow with nature, it can be practically left alone for years and still achieve its objective.

We have to look for ways of producing no waste, such as correctly building a compost pile and using that rich compost to build the soil in our gardens. We must actively place a value on diversity, remembering that for every caterpillar and aphid, there is a beneficial insect that depends on it for survival. We need to be willing to seek small, slow solutions, rather than reach for the nearest jug of surefire pesticide to solve a plant problem. And we can put our creativity and problem-solving skills to work by taking the time to observe patterns ("Hey, the cherry tree always blooms right after the tulips do!"), wisely using natural resources ("Maybe it's time to add a rainwater collection system?"), and helping nature along by actively encouraging diverse plants, birds, and insects to feel at home on our patches of land.

Another of the original principles of permaculture relates to food: "Obtain a yield." There are many different ways of putting this into practice. A remarkably simple one is to plant a fruit tree, ideally a fruit you dearly love. A healthy fruit tree provides pollen for mason bees, leaves for assorted caterpillars to munch, and roots for soil-dwelling grubs to hang around, in addition to preventing soil erosion—aside from the actual fruit you harvest each year. You can also obtain a yield from blueberry bushes or grapevines, a small vegetable plot, or herb pots on your balcony.

There is another way of thinking about yield, though. Who else are you feeding? The fruit of the serviceberry family of trees is not always delicious, but birds are happy to eat them, and the trees' early bloom time can be useful during years when pollinators are waking up before other fruit trees are blossoming. You may not enjoy eating nutrient-dense dandelion greens, but those sturdy plants are almost always a key source of nectar and pollen for the year's earliest bumble bees. Growing a plant that produces food, whether it is for you or an animal you appreciate, is an ongoing reminder of the life cycle of our gardens. Seeds become plants, plants become flowers, flowers become fruit, the fruit contains seeds, ultimately the plant itself will someday die—and different creatures depend on every stage of the plant's life and final decay. It is encouraging to see so many people looking for ways to protect, conserve, and encourage a new generation of healthy, thriving, polyculture gardens, both for people and for the pollinators that we depend on.

BEE MD

In early 2023, the USDA issued conditional approval for the first vaccine for honey bees, targeting the highly contagious American foulbrood created by *Paenibacillus larvae* bacteria. As of early 2024, it has limited availability in both the United States and Canada, primarily through the sale of inoculated queen bees. Developed by Dalan Animal Health and manufactured by Diamond Animal Health (owned by Heska Corporation), this vaccine gets mixed into feed for a hive's worker bees, which then mix it into royal jelly they feed to the hive's queen. As she digests the vaccine-laden royal jelly, some of the vaccine is deposited in her ovaries, which in turn provide larvae with immunity as they hatch.

POLLINATION SERVICES: WHAT THEY ARE AND HOW THEY WORK

While some farms maintain their own bee populations, it is much more common to rely on a pollination service. Pollination services take two basic forms:

- The hives stay put on a single farm year-round, and a *stationary service* maintains them. Some hives might be relocated a few times around the property over the course of the year, depending on the property's size.
- A *migratory service* brings in its own hives for a specific season (generally right before the orchard comes into bloom) and leaves once the crops have been pollinated and the blossoms are turning into tiny fruits. The hives are packed up and trucked on to the next crop, which is likely in a completely different state or province.

Bees That Stay Put

Stationary pollination services are typically found on small farms of 5–25 acres (2–10 hectares) that are growing several kinds of crops, including a mix of fruit trees and vegetables or flowers. The variety of plants offers food for the honey bees over many months (and also provides abundant food for wild bees on the property), and keeping the bees in the same place is less stressful for them. In some cases, the farmer pays the pollination service by the acre or per month; in others, it is by the number of hives maintained, or by a more complicated arrangement wherein the farmer sells honey and other bee products on behalf of the beekeeper and they share the proceeds.

Stationary pollinator services may be somewhat better for honey bees. (Slatan/Shutterstock)

An interesting, and fairly recent, development in the business of stationary pollination is that some beekeepers are now working only with farmers who are certified organic or who go beyond what the USDA organic standards require through one of several third-party-verified agricultural methods, such as Certified Naturally Grown. Other pollination companies merely demand that the farmer not spray certain chemicals on the crops while they are in flower (when the bees are visiting that specific crop), or they place specific limits on the categories of chemicals that can be used during the year. Chances are that these pollination companies will continue adjusting their guidelines for customers as more is learned about CCD and how different chemical herbicides, fungicides, and fertilizers affect the hives.

These stationary services appear to be at least somewhat more healthful for the honey bees in question, as long as the service routinely maintains the health of the hive. They can also be useful for the small-scale market farmer or urban farm-to-table chef who is already working incredibly long hours on their crops and does not have time to add honey beekeeping to their daily to-do list. However, they are not workable for the majority of farms in the United States, which focus on a single crop and need bees for only a few weeks each year. And when you have a farmer who not only grows a single crop but also grows it across multiple orchards that are each over 100 acres (40 hectares), you simply need more bees at one time than your local stationary pollinator company is going to be able to provide. This is where the migratory pollination companies fulfill a need.

WHY REGIONAL DROUGHTS MATTER FOR EVERYONE

California grows an astonishing amount of the food consumed in the United States: over 90 percent for crops as varied as garlic, artichokes, plums, walnuts, almonds, and kiwi fruit, and somewhat less, but still an incredible 80 percent, for grapes, broccoli, lettuce, cauliflower, and celery. The list continues through the grocery store aisles, including carrots, strawberries, asparagus, rice, pistachios, olives, and more. Soil and sunshine deserve much credit for the abundance, along with fast modes of transport to get these fresh ingredients spread from one coast throughout the country. Irrigation systems are also critical, and that is where we run up against a harsh meteorological reality: There is evidence that the five-to-seven-year droughts of the 20th century were only a tiny fraction of their potential length, as studies of tree rings indicate many droughts of over 20 years and two that were more than a century long. Thanks to two consecutive years of abnormally wet winters in 2022–2023, this key state got some short-term relief after about five years of increasingly ominous drought concerns and adjacent wildfires.

With the population growing dramatically in Arizona, New Mexico, and Texas, concerns about drought surrounding the Colorado River began making international headlines in early 2023. Between 2000 and 2021, the river lost an estimated 10 trillion gallons of water for reasons that relate to drought, population growth, and resource management across seven states. When this river's complex water rights were first written down, major considerations such as the area's Native communities' rights and the health of the river's ecosystem were simply not taken into account. Meanwhile, a cascade of "senior" and "junior" stakeholders have guaranteed rights that may not reflect their importance in the 21st century. As new legal documents are forged to boost equity in water access from this critical river, remember that residential lawn irrigation should be seen as one of the absolute lowest priorities—and if you live in an arid region that depends on a single river (either the Colorado or another), do what you can to educate your community about how thirsty lawn care can deprive healthy wild ecosystems of a key element.

The effects of a low food and water supply are already present in many parts of the Midwest and Southwest. Grasses are drying up and flowers are not blooming, or their bloom period is incredibly short. Salmon and kangaroo rats are dying in large numbers, deer and rabbits are being driven into farms and gardens (and being followed by their natural predators, including coyotes and mountain lions), and orphaned infant animals and distressed birds are appearing in large numbers at state animal shelters.

This is scary for our food supply and the financial stability of our farmers, with effects that could reach well beyond a single region. If California loses its ability to produce or distribute the food we currently rely on, the result will be high prices and scarcity for up to a decade, as other places work to ramp up production. With effort and cooperation, conservation efforts slow down the rapid changes in the wild environment and maintain irrigation to California farmland. Nonetheless, it reminds us that our food supply always needs a backup plan and that our own health is deeply tied to the health of myriad species.

BEES ON THE MOVE

The West Coast provides the perfect example of a place where the need exists for migratory pollination companies. The total number of almond-growing acres in California was estimated at 1.65 million acres (667,731 hectares) as of 2021, and the almond orchards typically bloom in February, while the fruit orchards

Imagine yourself experiencing this honey bee's life and you'll understand why being trucked all over North America is a worst-case scenario for a hive. (Christopher Bonis)

of Oregon and Washington are still dormant. The almond industry requires the efforts of numerous pollination services and honey bee brokerage companies to coordinate and ensure the delivery of approximately two beehives per acre (0.4 hectare) of California almond trees in bloom. That is an astonishing number of beehives, but remember that California grows 80 percent of all the almonds in the world today, and almonds are the largest (and possibly too large!) specialty crop export in the United States as of 2024. So many hives now start their year in almond orchards that almond honey is now making an appearance as a specialty food; it is savory and somewhat nutty, with an aftertaste that almost all tasters find at least slightly bitter. (Because of its flavor, it tends to cost less than other specialty honeys.)

After the almonds are done blooming, some hives will stay nearby to pollinate other California stone fruit crops (it might sound nutty to you, but an almond is a stone fruit, closely related to cherries and apricots). Others will be trucked farther north, as orchards begin blooming across the Pacific Northwest. As the months progress, the hives move from the stone fruit orchards to apple and pear orchards as well as to berry fields. No one industry needs as many hives at one time as almonds, but they are all greedy for pollination.

These mobile hives are the ones experiencing the largest percentage of bee die-off, and that is likely for a multitude of reasons. We've all learned how illness is spread in humans. The more sick people you come into even indirect contact with, the more likely you are to pick up a virus your immune system cannot fight off. Now imagine that you are already stressed out from a lot of recent travel and are trying to fight off that virus while living on food that is ever so slightly poisonous, all the while bringing that exposure to viruses, emotional stress, and unhealthy food home to your large family living in close quarters. Congratulations: You have imagined a honey bee's worst-case scenario, as your hive gets trucked around to orchards and fields that are being treated with chemicals, and where pollen from only one type of plant is available, sort of like humans trying to exist by sugary soda alone. And with the enormous range of each honey bee on their pollen-collecting route, each hive is basically Grand Central Terminal with no cleaning crew, where diseases are grossly easy to transmit. Sounds awful, doesn't it? It is clearly not a sustainable future—not for the bees and not for the farmers or beekeepers, who depend on well-pollinated crops and healthy pollinators for their livelihoods.

This worst-case scenario is what so many organizations and private companies are working to change, through a number of improvements. While farmers tend to be somewhat resistant to the adoption of new methods, they are ready and willing to accept rigorously proven evidence, even if it goes against a deeply held belief. It is obvious that too many honey bees have been mismanaged, and the numbers show that they are challenged. So when researchers are able to point toward specific chemicals like neonicotinoids as direct culprits in bee die-off, some farmers will look for ways to discontinue the use of these chemicals or to use them only at a time when pollination is not happening. Just as your home garden does not have to be 100 percent native species to help your local pollinators thrive, farms do not have to convert overnight to perfectly bee-safe practices in order to begin improving the health of migratory hives.

Once again, the remarkable flying range of honey bees is something everyone should think about—farmers, beekeepers, and you. Honey bees are such thoroughly efficient workers that it takes them a few hours to strip an orchard of its pollen. At that point, they do not call it a day and head off to happy hour. They fly farther from the hive in search of new sources of pollen. With a range of 2 miles (3.2 kilometers) or more per bee, this means that any chemicals recently sprayed within that distance can end up in the hive, where they will affect the entire community, even the bees not responsible for pollen or nectar collection.

The reality of this problem was highlighted in a study published in 2013 by the Public Library of Science, titled "Crop Pollination Exposes Honey Bees to Pesticides Which Alters Their Susceptibility to the Gut Pathogen *Nosema ceranae*."[5] In the different pollen samples collected, nine different pesticides and fungicides were present on average, an average that was skewed by one sample that contained a horrifying total of 21 agricultural chemicals. The authors identified eight chemicals associated with increased risk of parasitic infection, with fungicides being particularly problematic. This is alarming, as fungicide packaging does not warn farmers (or home gardeners) to avoid their use when pollinators are present.

This study made it clear that it is not simply a matter of what practices one orchard uses, or even a few orchards in close proximity. When 1.6 million hives are present, bees will be collecting pollen across dozens of miles, and every farm, garden, and park they encounter brings a risk of sending toxins back to the entire hive. Better labeling could help, as will stronger education efforts in agricultural communities. Most important will likely be the shift away from chemicals and in the direction of multiple pollinators working in concert.

A CLEAR CONNECTION: WHAT VALUE-ADDED PRODUCTS MEAN FOR FARMERS

At its simplest, a farm grows a food—let's say apples—and then sells those apples directly to people who will take the apples home and eat them. Easy enough, right? However, apples ripen in a relatively short window, typically August through October, and farmers need income for more than three months out of the year. Some varieties of apples go into storage and can be kept well chilled into the winter months, to be sold as fresh apples; that extends the income-earning months for our apple farmer from three months to five and highlights the importance of newer varieties like Cosmic Crisp, which was specifically bred for late ripening, good flavor, and a long shelf life. If the farmer is wise, and their climate supports it, they will grow a summer apple too, which might ripen in July.

That still leaves six months where they need to pay for labor in the orchard, along with taxes and living expenses, without direct income. There is also the simple problem that customers expect to (or need to) pay between $2 and $4 per pound ($6 to $10 CAD per kilogram) for fresh apples. The farmer will be paid much less than that, unless customers are buying directly from their farm stand—and most farm stands do not draw anywhere near enough customers to let a farmer sell 100 percent of their crop this way. Aside from this, customers—both the one who will bring that apple home to eat and the wholesale produce buyer for a grocery store—want apples that look a certain way: They need to be the right size, with attractive, blemish-free skin. Undersized or ugly apples might be absolutely delicious, but people tend to buy produce with their eyes.

Stories abound regarding food waste that is invisible to those who are not farmers or who do not live in farming communities. Apples that do not get precisely the right color may be thrown away. Cherries that are a tiny fraction (even 1/32 of an inch) too small for the packing houses do not have a secondary market; on average, Washington's cherry farmers lose about 25 percent of their annual crop because of this problem. And even with perfect fruit, there is always the risk of an infrastructure failure, such as the 2014–2015 labor slowdown at West Coast ports, which led to hundreds of airtight containers of fruit simply rotting. Nowadays, extreme summer heat and winter cold also lead to food loss each year, although which crops are affected changes.

To support farmers, seek out locally grown produce and value-added products, too. (Jill Lightner)

MEET THE BEES

Another way to reconnect with a key part of our food system is to take a class (both online or in person) or schedule a hive tour. Some companies and nonprofits highlight specific areas of interest, such as overcoming bee phobias (Half Mad Honey of Philadelphia, Pennsylvania) or exploring the intersection of pollination and religious faith (BeeVangelists of Milwaukee, Wisconsin). Opportunities in many urban areas across the country include "meeting the hives" during their months of activity, scheduling webinars for a group, or hosting a hive on commercial property. (See Resources for further information.)

Insurance covers only so much for these farmers, which can lead to terrible financial losses and in some cases the selling off of farmland to developers.

One solution is known as "value-added product" within the food industry, and the foods that are referred to this way are often the same that are disparaged as "processed food" by nutritionists and the media. If our apple farmer can fund their own projects and has a nearby customer base, they can buy a dehydrator to make apple chips; cook up delicious apple butter, syrup, and applesauce; or set up a juicing operation for fresh cider. Depending on the local laws, and if they have the time to invest, they might look into the hard-cider business or set up a still for making apple brandy; apple cider vinegar and pies or doughnuts are also possibilities.

Without access to funds or direct customers, however, they have to give up on the idea of adding value to foods themselves and look elsewhere, perhaps selling apples wholesale to a juice or cider company or selling the small or blemished apples, known as "peelers" in the industry, to corporations like McDonald's, which will then sell the inexpensive peeled and sliced apples as part of their kids' meals.

Value-added products have several huge benefits for farmers. First, they offer the possibility of year-round income, since they have a longer shelf life than, for example, fresh apples. Second, while customers expect prices on fresh produce to be low, they will cheerfully pay much more per pound for treats like sulfite-free dried apples, small-batch apple butter, or unfiltered apple cider. These items sell well at many farmers markets and upscale grocery stores or through online sources like Mercato, Goldbelly, Amazon, and ChefShop.

One way of reconnecting with food is to rethink your idea of what "processed food" means. Sure, mass-market snacks showered in high-sodium ranch-flavored powder are not a particularly direct means of supporting local agriculture or the health of your family. But paying a bit more for locally milled flour or seeking out a farmers market or farm stand the next time you are replenishing your jam supply are easy ways for you to help boost the income of your nearest farmers, while likely bringing a higher-quality "processed food" into your kitchen.

POLLINATOR SCIENCE

Primarily through the Farm Bill, which is a massive agriculture spending bill renewed (and fought over) by Congress every five years, the USDA helps fund programs targeted at farms

BEE DIRECT WITH HONEY AND SEED

While almost all value-added foods can be considered "bee adjacent," some are definitely closer to their pollinator sources than others. One of the ways we can all support bee-friendly agriculture is by limiting what honey we purchase and buying from small beekeepers who do not truck their bees around the continent but instead allow hives to remain on single farms (or sometimes, urban backyards). You can find unusual, single-varietal honeys in all sorts of food-centric shops across North America, including bakeries, delis, cheese shops, and gourmet grocers, from Granville Island, British Columbia, to the Ninth Ward of New Orleans, Louisiana. There are a number of nonprofit food justice organizations and a handful of Indigenous tribes that use revenue from honey sales to help fund nutrition, environmental, or employment programs that give back to their communities. If you'll be taking the honey home with you across an international border, make sure it does not include raw honeycomb, as import regulations typically do not allow that due to parasite concerns.

If your travel plans don't bring you into contact with these small producers, many are available online. Or look for alternative plant-based liquid sweeteners, as using them completely sidesteps the honey question and reduces the harm and stress that honey bees may experience. (See Resources for a few options.)

Seed companies offer another way of bringing unusual varietals into your garden and pantry. Small companies do exist, but it's unlikely you'll find their products at a hardware chain. And, while a special honey will taste the same in every kitchen, a special seed may not grow as well at your home as it does where you admire the plant on your vacation. Still, curious gardeners can source interesting shelling beans, unusual heirloom vegetables, or wildflowers in seed form, while supporting small and medium-sized companies and nonprofits or seed collectives along the way. As with honeycomb products, trying to bring seeds across international borders isn't recommended, this time because of concerns about invasive plants. (See Resources for options.)

Wildflower meadows are just one example of pollinator-friendly habitats. (Barbara Smits/Shutterstock)

using large-scale pollination. These long-term Conservation Reserve Programs (CRPs) provide financial incentives for farmers who remove "environmentally sensitive land from agricultural production and plant species that will improve environmental health and quality."[6] This land includes grasslands, forests, and many types of buffer areas near watersheds. As of 2023, the total CRP-enrolled acreage has reached 24.8 million acres (10.3 million hectares).

The USDA publishes a Strategic Pollinator Priorities Report each year, which compiles information from research grants, conservation programs, and agricultural business data, including a key partnership: the EPA and the Tribal Pesticide Program Council (TPPC), which represents a network of nearly three dozen Native tribes. According to the preamble of the 2022 report, "The EPA Office of Chemical Safety and Pollution Prevention and the TPPC formed a workgroup to address pollinator protection, and one of the workgroup's goals is to collaborate with USDA to provide input to this report on pollinator research priorities from the Tribal perspective."[7]

It may sound like dry government-speak, but the report does a tremendous job of acknowledging how interconnected the health of our thousands of wild pollinator species is with the health of North America's pollinator industry, food system, and wild lands. Research data is being streamlined and made more accessible, pest and pathogen tracking is being standardized, and commercial interests are being balanced against habitat restoration goals. A sizable portion of the 2022 report calls attention to information gaps and an enormous need for further study, particularly when it comes to our wild and solitary pollinator friends.

It's not only the USDA and EPA that are interested in the health of pollinators. Other US federal agencies with a pollinator-centered component include the Department of Transportation (working to improve habitat along highways), the Department of Energy (protecting and planting for pollinators on massive swaths of land otherwise devoted to our power grid), and the Department of Defense (which prefers areas of diverse native planting for military training exercises and has conducted surveys and studies on pollinators since the early 1990s). Check out the landing page for the 2022 report (usda.gov/pollinators) and fall into a delightful rabbit hole of discovery.

In Canada, much of the readily available national information on pollinators focuses on commercial pesticides and their potential impacts; each province hosts a telephone hotline[8] to call if you encounter a situation where you suspect pollinators are being poisoned. One national nonprofit is Wildlife Preservation Canada, whose work includes habitat and species restoration across the country, with both regional and international partners. In addition to funding the work of others, their projects include monitoring more than a dozen sites in Ontario for wild pollinator health and working to restore the Taylor's checkerspot butterfly to the Fraser River through a caterpillar breeding program and habitat improvement.

It's clear that North America has learned that no pollinator exists in a bubble and that healthy ecosystems include agricultural land. Particularly as government agencies address issues of climate change head-on, there's a drive to manage the research itself and the quick spread of results as efficiently as possible.

GETTING SOLITARY BEES ONTO FARMS

We do not recommend passing along cocoons directly to your favorite farmer at a farmers market; in the first few seasons, farmers (and their mason and leaf bees) tend to need some hand-holding. Farmers are experts with their crops: They know how to prune, how to graft, how to apply which chemicals, when to bring in extra labor, when to harvest, and when it is finally time to (briefly) relax. However, for one thing, they are not likely to have the right kind of soil to be a mason bee host and might need some supplemental clay. They will also likely need some education on the life cycle of the bee that will be in their orchard for six weeks, and they may have questions along the way. If you give your bees to a farmer who nonchalantly tries to introduce them into an orchard without any knowledge or expertise, they will almost certainly be unsuccessful. And remember that failure spreads like wildfire, while success is shared with friends.

CONNECTING THE DOTS: FARM TO GARDEN TO FARM

As farmers work to improve their practices and researchers strive to investigate effective alternatives, or additions, to the work done by honey bees, you can also find various ways to change your bee-havior. One of the easiest ways is to simply have conversations with people about bees, particularly ones that focus on solutions rather than troubles. Another way is to carefully consider what the best use for your own extra cocoons is.

As we have shown, raising your own solitary bees takes minimal effort. Nonetheless, the extra steps we have outlined of harvesting cocoons

Like tomatoes? Get bees to boost your yield of heirloom and non-heirloom varieties alike. (Courtesy of Seattle Department of Neighborhoods P-Patch Program)

and checking for parasites or other problems, along with using the proper sort of bee house, can make a big difference in the population over a few short seasons. It is a bit like taking care of a yard: Once established, most plants can nearly take care of themselves, but how much healthier are the plants if you do occasional pruning, watering, and basic maintenance? Bulbs do better if they are dug up every few years and divided—either moved around to additional areas of your yard or shared with a friend. You will see the same point reached after a year or two with mason bees, which is why we encourage you to plan ahead and think about what you will be able to do when you have cocoons to share. Crown Bees' Bee Buy Back program (see Resources) offers a possible solution.

Once you begin observing and tending to pollinators, and growing even a small amount of food, you will discover a new appreciation for the astonishing amount of effort it takes to get food on the table. The back-to-the-land movement, as well as the more recent farm-to-table movement, have both focused on what were seen as simpler lives, or at least simpler ways of eating. The truth is, little about food is simple. Layers upon layers of biological and botanical systems are required to create healthy garden soil, and numerous insects, birds, and mammals must work together to create the thriving and functional ecosystem that we refer to as a farm or garden. When one part of the system is thrown out of balance by changes in climate, plant disease, or loss of pollinators, the entire system is suddenly threatened. The food supply needs to be protected, but to do so both quickly and sustainably will take the concerted efforts of everyone involved.

CHAPTER 8

BEE-HOLD THE FUTURE: SOLITARY BEES, FOOD, AND WHAT COMES NEXT

Since about 2010, the plight of the honey bee has become fairly common knowledge; even people who do not know much about the specifics have at least heard there is trouble. Fast-forward a decade, when that meme darling, the northern giant hornet, grabbed attention, unfortunately detracting from invasive species with more immediate relevance. What we would like to see is the same meme-able, widespread awareness of the power of mason bees, leaf bees, and other species of solitary bees around the world—and what that power can mean for our food supply and related ecosystems.

FOUR BEE-DAZZLING POLLINATOR RESEARCH PROJECTS

For years, pollinator research focused heavily on honey bees, but these projects look to other species for a broader perspective.

1. Unlocking Leaf Bee Generations

According to Dr. Theresa Singer, many US alfalfa seed farmers have to purchase new alfalfa leafcutter bees from Canada each year, while Canada produces the bees in surplus. Comparing bees raised in Utah with those raised in Saskatchewan, researchers have learned that the length of the sunlight hours on the queen bees is key to their eggs either developing into an adult in a few weeks or overwintering in the larval stage—but it's not the only piece of the puzzle. Along with maturation speed, it matters how much food gets prepared for each egg. Conclusions in a 2022 master's thesis by Utah State University student Makenna Johnson stated that "mother bees in poor condition were much more likely to make small provision masses for their offspring, which led to more of them becoming non-diapausers [hatch in a few weeks]."[1] Singer explained, "All of this line of research helps us understand why [alfalfa leafcutter bees] in the United States compared to those in Canada are more likely to become adults in the summer of their birth rather than to remain in cocoons for the winter so they are available as commercial pollinators in the next year."[2]

2. Building Better Boxes

The Dyce Lab for Honey Bee Studies at Cornell University is focused on understanding how pesticides, pathogens, and habitat impact the health of honey bees and native wild pollinators. One study, authored by Olivia Miller and colleagues, first published in February 2023, looked at how commercial bumble bee boxes impacted wild bumble bee populations. It demonstrated a devastating problem for wild bumble bees, where larger species viewed the specific wild species as potential hive burglars. Titled "Commercial *Bombus impatiens* Colonies Function as Ecological Traps for Wild Queens,"[3] this study showed quite plainly the need for a simple device called a queen excluder. Without the excluders, "an average of 10 dead wild queens were recovered from each standard colony during the two-week period of the experiment, but colonies with queen excluders were successful in preventing wild queen deaths." At the same time, these excluders didn't create negative impacts for the commercial colonies. Lab manager Dr. Scott McArt contacted the two vendors of commercial bumble bee hive boxes in North America shortly before the paper published, and Ontario-based Plant Products began using the excluders immediately, as their bee boxes shipped out for spring pollination.

3. Long-Term Data Analysis

Sometimes, a pollinator study doesn't set out to collect new data but instead combines and analyzes the results of previous research projects. Such is the case with the alarmingly titled 2022 paper "Recent and Future Declines of a Historically Widespread Pollinator Linked to Climate, Land Cover, and Pesticides," written by more than a dozen authors who work in both the United States and Canada. Together, they mapped out a few possible futures for the formerly common, wide-ranging western bumble bee, focusing on the key factors that join forces for the success—or the failure—of the species. The authors make the case that when a successful generalist species is failing, there is even greater cause for concern when it comes to specialists (which focus on one particular plant species, rather than many), writing, "By the 2050s, our most optimistic scenario predicts occupancy declines in almost half of ecoregions; more severe scenarios predict declines in all ecoregions ranging from 51 to 97 percent. The precipitous decline of this generalist species is a bellwether for loss across many taxa sensitive to environmental changes around the globe."[4]

4. Mapping the Mason Bee Genome
Mason bees have two periods of dormancy in their lives. Once in the heat of summer shortly after their mother created their eggs, and again in the winter, before they are ready to emerge and begin pollinating and creating their next generation. Researchers in North Dakota and Spain wrote, "The life cycle of *O. lignaria* provides a unique opportunity to compare the physiological and molecular mechanisms underlying two ecologically contrasting dormancies within the same species. . . . To compare these two dormancies, we measured metabolic rates and gene expression across development as bees initiate, maintain, and terminate both prepupal (summer) and adult (overwintering) dormancies."[5] The expectation is that going forward, additional researchers will be able to use this information as they continue to learn how environments and locations during the dormant stages impact when the adults are ready to emerge. Such information will potentially allow humans to manipulate the species for precise, crop-specific utility.

Once you have begun keeping mason or leaf bees, you are automatically a fantastic person to help spread the news, as you will have witnessed firsthand how easy raising them is and what their impact has been on your garden and backyard harvest. Along with that, you will be familiar with the steps you had to take to convert your yard into a thriving bee haven, so you will have a good idea or two to share when a neighbor asks what they might be able to do to improve their own yard, whether it relates to the soil, the plants, or the gardening practices.

Still, it can be hard to stay inspired when you are the only person among your acquaintances who knows what a solitary bee is. People are decidedly not solitary bees; we are highly social creatures who crave connection. It is those connections—the conversations at work or as you go about your day—that have the greatest chance of helping you stay interested in your bees. Those human interactions can also provide you with the inspiration to go beyond your own backyard and bee-vangelize on behalf of your solitary bees of either species and the joys of creating a pollinator-friendly habitat.

FINDING COMMUNITY

Farmers have a number of organizations they can belong to for the exchange of information. Some are as education focused as 4H, some as

Mixed habitats like this one in a park can be useful props to educate humans about pollinators and other wildlife. (Jill Lightner)

massive in scale as state growers associations or fruit commissions (such as the Almond Board of California or Northwest Cherries), and some cover even larger geographical areas but are only relevant to a specific set of interests or farming practices, such as the Midwest Organic Services Association or Tilth Producers of Washington. Through newsletters, seasonal conferences, and annual meetings, information is passed along and members are kept current on topics that are relevant to their region or primary crop.

On a smaller scale, home honey beekeepers have connected with local apiary clubs to learn the tools of the trade and can readily access information on how to deal with a swarm or what the local regulations are for those who might be interested in setting up a hive. There is also the instant community found through shopping for plants at independently owned garden centers, which sometimes offer classes and educational newsletters, host meetings for the garden club chapter, or bring in Master Gardeners to offer advice throughout the year.

In comparison, it is a little harder for bee haven gardeners and mason beekeepers to find each other. Perhaps solitary bees attract more solitary people, but we believe the real difficulty lies in the generally low awareness of these gentle bees. We are part of a growing movement to boost awareness and community among mason and leaf beekeepers, who take advantage of the internet to connect across sometimes large distances.

THE HIVE MIND

The Orchard Bee Association (orchardbee.org) hosts an annual conference for members and sends out periodic newsletters. It earned 501(c)(3) nonprofit status in 2014, and its official goal is "to accelerate the production and use of orchard mason bees in various spring crops and orchards."

The association works to connect those with any level of commercial or academic interest in furthering this goal, whether they are students, beekeepers, farmers, or scientists; members come to the conference from all over the world. The newsletter showcases this mix of academia and commercial practitioners, offering laypeople's takes on recent studies or newly published research efforts, along with brief glimpses directly into ongoing research via studious updates directly from the participating researchers.

In 2015, a plethora of national organizations, plant societies, and garden clubs teamed up to create the Million Pollinator Garden Challenge (millionpollinatorgardens.org), which offered a casual way of connecting your efforts with the work of others. This campaign aimed to register a million gardens, parks, and landscaping projects that are pollinator friendly; click the map and you might find anything from a massive corporation (several Microsoft campuses were registered) to a national forest to a family-owned restaurant with an herb garden to an unnamed hobbyist. This goal was surpassed in less than four years. According to the National Wildlife Federation, their Garden for Wildlife participants contributed about one-third of the million-plus gardens; the total amount of new or enhanced pollinator habitat was around five million acres (2 million hectares).

A little over one month after the announcement that the Million Pollinator Garden Challenge had been a success, in January 2019, Monarch Watch (monarchwatch.org) reported a 144 percent increase in the population of the eastern monarch, a species that had been struggling for years. Unfortunately, there was not enough done to create lasting success, and as of winter 2024, the population that overwinters in Mexico was the second smallest on record. While it's easy for butterfly fans to be discouraged, remember that pollinator gardens benefit all sorts of insects, which in turn can benefit the birds, amphibians, and mammals that share their ecosystem. It is worth keeping at it.

In Canada, the Pollinator Partnership (pollinatorpartnership.ca) offers a training program to earn certification as a Pollinator Steward. The 10-hour program can be completed online, in person, or as a hybrid mix and covers topics such as identifying and monitoring pollinators, techniques for habitat enhancement, and the local Native perspective, including relevant ancient knowledge, culture, and history. The organization also manages a wealth of community science projects, gathering data for bumble bee and butterfly populations across Canada.

Education or formal certification on basic pollinator-friendly practices for gardeners or landscaping services to implement is a way of stretching beyond caring for a single species. Practices such as providing a water source for pollinators, growing pollen-laden plants in generously sized "pollinator target" clumps that include some native species, eliminating (or sternly minimizing) pesticides of all kinds, and striving for continuous bloom throughout the growing season are methods that show results across many species, in many regions.

TOP 10 WAYS TO MAKE YOUR COMMUNITY BEE-LOVED

Every community is filled with spaces and people ready to welcome bees or revise their policies to become friendlier to pollinators. There are many ways to put your skills and expertise in this realm to work.

1. **Reach out to farmers markets.** Farmers market shoppers have an interest in the health of the local food supply, which means they are invested in the health of local pollinators. Many market organizations will let you, perhaps with the help of a few bee-loving friends, set up an educational table to talk about your bees, explain how easy they are to care for, and offer free handouts on pollinator-friendly gardening practices and mason or leaf beekeeping.

DR. SHAWN A. STEFFAN

ASSOCIATE PROFESSOR, UNIVERSITY OF WISCONSIN–MADISON, AND RESEARCH ENTOMOLOGIST, USDA

Dr. Steffan has worked as an entomologist since 1994. His early-2020s area of research offers something of a correction to the average bee-curious gardener, who likely assumes that their spring and summer diet of nectar and pollen means that most bees are vegan. In an email, he wrote, "Bees are omnivores. Seriously, they eat a lot of meat. The meat, in this case, is typically microbial meat. Virtually all bees are omnivorous because the microbes they eat are herbivores."

Microbes come up frequently around the topic of human digestion and diet. If you've ever had a doctor talk to you about your gut, or you've played around with sourdough, microbes are inherently part of the conversation. Most commonly, they're bacteria that are heavily involved in fermentation. As you adjust components in your diet or your starter recipe for better balance, you probably don't think of yourself as a farmer—but maybe you should.

The idea of insects as farmers is something many gardeners have come across—as with ants "farming" aphids. These tiny animals have a close relationship of mutual benefit, called symbiosis or mutualism, and humans may see that relationship play out in our gardens. Steffans broadens this concept, writing, ". . . bees farm microbes, and by that same token, microbes are bee keepers. It's a symbiosis, and as such, both symbiont groups need the other to various degrees. Without one, the other struggles. It's two interacting communities, though—not the old canonical one-on-one species-for-species relationship. When we're talking about communities, we're talking about many species within each group. . . . It also amazed me the degree to which microbes support so many plants and animals. They're the 'silent third partners' of most mutualisms. As a species, a microbial population can benefit tremendously from a mutualism, even though a portion of their population becomes prey as the cost of the 'partnership.'"

How does it work at this microscopic community level? Steffans is able to simplify it:

"Microbes are on/in the flowers and on/in the adult bee as they forage. Bees gather pollen and nectar, mix them, curate them within a safe space [like a nest], and inoculate the blend with microbes as they are provisioning their baby bees. The microbes proliferate and become nutritious 'livestock' for the larval bees. Of course, the adult bees don't know they're inoculating the microbes—the bees just collect the pollen and nectar, and their microbial symbionts colonize it. Some portion of the microbes can survive and thrive in the bee gut. These are symbionts, too, and they help to further break down the pollen grains for the bees."

Steffan's work directly connects and measures "the degree to which microbes have eaten a substrate, and the degree to which animals have eaten the microbes." (To translate for the hobbyist, picture a commercial orchard spraying a fungicide at night, when no bees are present. That spray can still impact bees because the fungicide has altered microbes in the pollen on the blooms that were sprayed.) It presents new considerations for gardening practices, regardless of the plants grown or the size of the garden, and you don't have to be a microbiologist to wrap your head around the ideas. If you're already used to the idea of "gut health" for yourself, it's easy to make the leap in thinking about the gut health of the community of insects visiting your flowers for pollen and its microbes. Similarly, if you're one of the multitude of sourdough enthusiasts, you already have some understanding of how things like feeding your starter an ounce of rye flour can create dramatic action.

The same types of seemingly minor choices—such as planting a few too many modern hybrid flowers or spraying once for a fungus when pollinators are active—can create microbial effects that may have lasting repercussions that appear considerably after your action, perhaps in the next generation of bees, or perhaps in the microscopic food they farm and collect for their own offspring. It's sobering, but it doesn't have to be alarming. Think of it as microbial food for thought.

2. **Visit with Master Gardeners.** Affiliated with university extension programs across the United States, Master Gardeners invest a lot of effort in their training, and many of them can be found at nurseries and hardware stores offering free expertise on gardening. Many tend to have a special area of interest; you might meet one who knows everything about roses and nothing about fruit trees, then have a different encounter in which the reverse is true. However, extension programs host regular discussions on topics that relate to almost all areas of gardening, and you might meet with current students in search of a project to assist on to complete their certification. Their interests are a natural fit with those of mason and leaf beekeepers; it only needs a little outreach.
3. **Join your neighborhood's landscaping board.** Many planned communities have HOA rules that govern street-facing landscaping, which can make it difficult to plant native species or add bee-friendly plants. Some might even require annual pest

spraying and pay for it out of homeowners' dues! The best way to change these rules is not to fight them from the outside, since you might end up with grumpy neighbors or a fine for not following the design codes. Instead, join the board or oversight committee and, by educating your fellow members, help change the rules one step at a time. A beautiful yard can have a meadow of flowers adjacent to a small patch of green lawn and still keep everyone happy.

4. **Turn your place of worship's garden space into a pollinator habitat.** The activities of digging a garden, tending plants, and welcoming little creatures to the new environment around your temple, church, or synagogue are great ways to foster community and enjoy some outdoor time with others in the congregation. Get children involved—or, if the organization also runs a school or daycare, chat with the principal to see if there is a way for the students to participate.
5. **Start or expand a community garden program.** While many cities are expanding their community garden programs, there is often a waiting list for a space. In some cases, it is up to the local parks department to identify the desire in a specific neighborhood and reassign land from whatever its previous use was to become new garden beds. If the community does not make its voice heard, the department will not know the interest exists! If your area does not yet have such a program, check with your local government to see how you might go about starting one; in many cases it takes only a little grassroots activism. You can learn about many existing gardens across the United States and in Canada at Communitygarden.org.
6. **Plant or maintain an urban orchard.** Community orchards are less common than community gardens, but the movement is growing. In some cases, land with an existing orchard is donated to the parks department. Sometimes, new orchards get planted: Seattle's Beacon Food Forest was already making international headlines shortly after the new 7-acre (2.8-hectare) permaculture project was approved by the city. Its first funding, for planning and design, came through a neighborhood grant in 2010, and groundbreaking took place in 2012. By their 10th anniversary, they had harvested thousands of pounds of fruit, vegetables, and nuts (some of the harvest was donated to community food banks), planted a native plant garden in a restored wetland, and begun a

Community gardens are a natural place for leaf bees and can help boost food production. (PeopleImages.com/Shutterstock)

Encouraging children to appreciate bees helps them begin to learn how food is grown. (Courtesy of Seattle Department of Neighborhoods P-Patch Program)

BIPOC Community Garden, with the goal "to grow culturally relevant foods, medicines, and herbs for people of color." While gardens of this scope remain rare, check around for your nearest orchard and offer to contribute and maintain a mason bee box—or take inspiration from the Beacon Food Forest and kickstart a similar project in your own community.

7. **Speak about mason bees at a local school.** Teachers are appreciative when experts are willing to share their expertise with a class. Find out if an elementary school teacher or middle school science teacher would enjoy having you visit. Right before you plan to put your bees out for the year is a great time, as you can easily bring a few cocoons and nesting tubes with you. For high school or community college, see if there is a horticulture class that would benefit or if pollinators are being covered in botany or biology. You never know where an interest in pollinators might appear! If you dread public speaking, see about developing a written handout for the teacher to share or work with a friend who enjoys it on a joint presentation.
8. **Support land conservation in your region.** There are many kinds of land trusts and conservation programs that would benefit pollinators through your financial support. These trusts buy parcels of land and see that they are permanently held only for specific uses. Typically, these uses are either organic farming, wild habitat, or a mixture, and you can find them operating at every level from county to federal. They are usually run by private foundations and not government agencies, but some are

BEENOME100

A USDA work-in-progress is expected to assist bee research in countless ways. Announced in 2022, the Beenome100 project is working to genetically sequence 100 bee species through a sizable collaboration of many government and university researchers in the United States. In its first year, 54 high-priority species were collected and sequenced, including bees at risk of extinction. According to a statement from the USDA, "Once a genome is mapped, the data becomes publicly available [online via the National Agricultural Library] for scientists to work on the next step: linking functions to specific genes."[6] It is likely that this will then allow humans to both support bees more effectively and genetically manipulate them. Updates are available at Beenome.org.

public-private partnerships or are based on tribal land. (See Resources for websites that will help you find land trusts in your part of the country.)

9. **Buy plants from your local native plant society.** While the majority of nurseries likely carry a small selection of native plants, going directly to the source for your plant starts can get you a larger variety to choose from while at the same time supporting valuable education and preservation programs. Most regional societies hold one or more plant sales during the course of a year, but spring is the most common time. Some offer native trees for sale during the fall.
10. **Give the gift of bees.** Aside from giving bee houses and cocoons as housewarming gifts to neighbors (they are also the perfect gift for the gardener who already has everything but mason bees), you can find opportunities to scatter them around the community. Donate a kit to your school or favorite nonprofit's silent auction. Donate books about them and pollinator-friendly gardening methods to your city or county library. If a nearby restaurant you love has a kitchen garden or rooftop deck where they grow plants, offer a bee house to the restaurateur. The same idea would be fun for a grocery co-op or anywhere else that supports growing food.

FOOD ON THE TABLE

The relationship between humans and pollinators has always been a somewhat selfish one on our part—perhaps not as blindly selfish as bears robbing hives for honeycomb, but the sort of uneven relationship in which we gained far more from bees than they gained from us. That idea was neglected in the late 20th century, but it has rebounded in the first half of the 21st, with a new, friendlier spin. We may have set out to save the honey bee and the monarch, but the process opened our eyes to a long list of pollinating animals.

Every creature needs food to live, whether it is a ball of pollen and nectar that keeps a mason bee larva alive for eight months, or the nourishing breakfast we want kids to eat to start their day. Without us, wild bees are perfectly capable of finding food and have been doing so for thousands of years. But the reverse is not true: Without bees, we will be hard-pressed to feed ourselves.

Happily, raising your own bees is far easier than raising your own food. There is no successful vegetable garden or fruit orchard that requires as little effort from you as a mason bee house. It is also easier for you to spread mason bees around your community than it was for John Chapman (a.k.a. Johnny Appleseed) to spread his famous apple trees. With mason bees, the simple, seasonal activities that lead to success do not take long at all and can be done with a friend as part of educating them about bees.

In 1928, Herbert Hoover ran for president on a famous campaign promise: "A chicken in every pot, and a car in every garage." That promise collapsed in the spectacular failure of the Great Depression, but the image of prosperity it offered turned "a chicken in every pot" into a cliché that lingers as we near a century since its introduction. A more active way of thinking about abundant food is not a miraculously available pot of chicken stew for all, but a mason bee house for every home or apartment building. Imagine if every dwelling in your neighborhood had a patch of bee-friendly plants and a small bee house with a few dozen bees. Doesn't that sound like something that can boost food production?

There is an idea promoted by conservancy groups called a "keystone species," a term originally developed by Robert T. Paine when he was a professor at the University of Washington. It refers to a species that has a disproportionately large effect on the ecosystem it inhabits. A good example of the concept's use is to cite the North American beaver to support the idea of protecting both forest and watershed as a whole. Officially, most farms are not true ecosystems; they are too carefully engineered, and even manipulated, by humans to deserve the title. But in regenerative or permaculture farming, a complete ecosystem is the goal, as it is in your backyard bee haven. Every single pollinator may not technically meet the definition of a keystone species, but as a unified whole, pollinators are absolutely necessary and merit our careful and sustained attention.

When we talk generally about "saving the bees," we often talk about what we need to do—fewer toxins of all kinds, more wild habitat and native species—but we rarely speak about the grim reality of why it is so important to humanity. It boils down to this: Effective pollinators of every kind are essential when it comes to our food supply. By saving them, we save ourselves.

ACKNOWLEDGMENTS

Creating this second edition has been a journey made possible by many generous and talented people.

First, my heartfelt thanks to Jill Lightner, whose exceptional writing skills helped shape this book into something accessible, compelling, and grounded in science. You made the words sing.

To Janet, Kate, and everyone at Mountaineers Books: Thank you for your patience with my ever-busy life at Crown Bees. Your flexibility and gentle nudging kept me on track through (most) every deadline.

To the Crown Bees team: You are the backbone of this mission. Albert, Maddi, and Tina, thank you for your tireless work building and shipping our products, carefully handling bees from fall through summer, and ensuring our books stay accurate and up to date. Your dedication is extraordinary. I'm especially grateful to Kelly and Julie, whose thoughtful insights and creative energy have been invaluable sounding boards as we continue to innovate and explore new paths forward.

Science is vital to the future of humanity. The entomologists and bee labs working behind the scenes deserve our full support. The USDA/ARS Logan Bee Lab, (Theresa, Jim, Lindsie, Diana) in particular, deserves a standing ovation for their years of dedication to understanding solitary bees. Their research continues to reveal hidden treasures that help our fuzzy friends survive all that humanity sends their way.

This book, like our work, is a collective effort. Thank you all for believing in the power of small bees to make a big difference.

—Dave Hunter

Many thanks to all who took the time to answer my questions about their work, in particular Wendy Caldwell, Joe Dlugo, Dr. Theresa Singer, and Dr. Shawn Steffan. Appreciation to Kate, Janet, and the team at Mountaineers Books—it is remarkable that an independent publisher continues to exist, and I'm proud to be one of your authors. Thank you to federally funded programs that make North America safer for pollinators and people and to the Duwamish River Community Coalition for their ongoing efforts where I live and work. Thanks to Rachelle for my beautiful walking stick and to the medical team that works to keep my disabled body functional. To all my friends who text me blurry photos of bugs in the hope that I can identify them for you: I still cannot, beyond "That is definitely a bug of some sort!" But I still like getting your texts. My lifelong gratitude to every single librarian and anyone who has ever contributed to or voted on behalf of libraries—our world would be both more boring and more ignorant in their absence.

—Jill Lightner

NOTES

INTRODUCTION

1. M. Shahbendah, "Leading Producers of Natural Honey Worldwide in 2023," Statista, accessed January 23, 2025, www.statista.com/statistics/812172/global-top-producers-of-honey/.
2. "The African Bee-Keeping Story," Norton Rose Fulbright, February 2016, https://nortonrosefulbright.com/en/knowledge/publications/7515691a/the-african-bee-keeping-story.
3. Martina Gajardo-Rojas, Ariel A. Muñoz, Jonathan Barichivich, et al., "Declining Honey Production and Beekeeper Adaptation to Climate Change in Chile," *Progress in Physical Geography: Earth and Environment* 46, no. 5 (2022): 737–756, https://doi.org/10.1177/03091333221093757.
4. Nathalie Steinhauer, "United States Honey Bee Colony Losses 2022–23: Preliminary Results from the Bee Informed Partnership," Bee Culture: The Magazine of American Beekeeping (August 7, 2023), https://beeculture.com/study-hall-3/.

CHAPTER 1

1. M. D. Levin and M. H. Haydak, "Comparative Value of Different Pollens in the Nutrition of *Osmia lignaria*," *Bee World* 38, no. 9 (1957): 221–226, https://doi.org/10.1080/00057 72X.1957.11095007.
2. Jordi Bosch, William P. Kemp, and Glen E. Trostle, "Bee Population Returns and Cherry Yields in an Orchard Pollinated with *Osmia lignaria* (Hymenoptera: Megachilidae)," *Journal of Economic Entomology* 99, no. 2 (April 2006): 408–413, https://doi.org/10.1603/0022-0493-99.2.408.
3. Claire Brittain, Neal Williams, Claire Kremen, and Alexandra-Maria Klein, "Synergistic Effects of Non-*Apis* Bees and Honey Bees for Pollination Services," *Proceedings of the Royal Society B* 280 (March 7, 2013), https://doi.org/10.1098/rspb.2012.2767.
4. Kit Prendergast, Philip W. Bateman, and Kingsley W. Dixon, "The Evidence For and Against Competition Between the European Honeybee and Australian Native Bees," *Pacific*

Conservation Biology 29, no. 2 (March 2022), https://doi.org/10.1071/PC21064; Maureen L. Page and Neal M. Williams, "Evidence of Exploitative Competition Between Honey Bees and Native Bees in Two California Landscapes," *Journal of Animal Ecology* 92, no. 9 (September 2023): 1802–1814, https://doi.org/10.1111/1365-2656.13973.

CHAPTER 4

1. W. S. Cranshaw, "Leafcutter Bees," fact sheet no. 5.576, Colorado State University Extension, https://extension.colostate.edu/docs/pubs/insect/05576.pdf.
2. Oregon State University, "Wild Bees Flock to Forested Areas Affected by Severe Fire," *Science Daily*, April 3, 2019, www.sciencedaily.com/releases/2019/04/190403094132.htm.

CHAPTER 5

1. Center for Agriculture, Food, and the Environment, UMass Extension Fruit Program, "Protecting Honeybees & Native Pollinators," University of Massachusetts–Amherst, https://ag.umass.edu/fruit/ne-small-fruit-management-guide/appendices-resource-material-listings-conversion-tables-0.

CHAPTER 6

1. Thomas Renaud and Meredith Root-Bernstein, "Flower Visitor Insects Display an Interspecific Dominance Hierarchy on Flowers," *Ecology: Ecology Society of America* 104, no. 3 (March 2023): e3958, https://doi.org/10.1002/ecy.3958.
2. Communications and Publishing, "White-Nose Syndrome Killed over 90% of Three North American Bat Species," US Geological Survey, April 21, 2021, https://usgs.gov/news/national-news-release/white-nose-syndrome-killed-over-90-three-north-american-bat-species.

CHAPTER 7

1. Statistics Canada/Statistique Canada, "Canada's Fastest Growing and Decreasing Municipalities from 2016 to 2021," Government of Canada, February 9, 2022, www12.statcan.gc.ca/census-recensement/2021/as-sa/98-200-x/2021001/98-200-x2021001-eng.cfm.
2. "Large Southern Cities Lead Nation in Population Growth," press release CB23-79, US Census Bureau, May 18, 2023, https://census.gov/newsroom/press-releases/2023/subcounty-metro-micro-estimates.html.
3. Natural Agricultural Statistics Service, "Census of Agriculture," US Department of Agriculture, 2022, https://nass.usda.gov/Publications/AgCensus/2022/index.php.
4. Dave Whitinger and Relevant Insights for National Gardening Association, "National Gardening Survey: 2024 Edition," National Gardening Association, 2024, https://gardenresearch.com.
5. Jeffery S. Pettis, Elinor M. Lichtenberg, Michael Andree, Jennie Stitzinger, Robyn Rose, and Dennis vanEngelsdorp, "Crop Pollination Exposes Honey Bees to Pesticides Which Alters Their Susceptibility to the Gut Pathogen *Nosema ceranae*," *PLOS ONE* 8, no. 7 (2013): e70182, https://doi.org/10.1371/journal.pone.0070182.
6. Conservation Reserve Program, https://www.nrcs.usda.gov/programs-initiatives/crp-conservation-reserve-program.
7. 2022 Strategic Pollinator Priorities Report, USDA, June 2022, https://www.usda.gov/sites/default/files/documents/annual-pollinator-report-2022.pdf.

8. Government of Canada, "Pollinator Protection," https://canada.ca/en/health-canada/services/consumer-product-safety/pesticides-pest-management/growers-commercial-users/pollinator-protection.html.

CHAPTER 8

1. Makenna May Johnson, "Maternal Effects and Management of Alfalfa Leafcutting Bees" (Thesis, Utah State University, 2022), Digital Commons, Utah State University, https://digitalcommons.usu.edu/etd/8558.
2. Theresa L. Pitts-Singer, "Photoperiod Effect on *Megachile rotundata* (Hymenoptera: Megachilidae) Female Regarding Diapause Status of Progeny: The Importance of Data Scrutiny," *Environmental Entomology* 49, no. 2 (April 2020): 516–527, https://doi.org/10.1093/ee/nvaa004.
3. Olivia Miller, Casey Hale, Leeah Richardson, et al., "Commercial *Bombus impatiens* Colonies Function as Ecological Traps for Wild Queens," *Journal of Applied Ecology* 60, no. 4 (April 2023): 592–600, https://doi.org/10.1111/1365-2664.14353.
4. William M. Janousek, Margaret R. Douglas, Syd Cannings, et al., "Recent and Future Declines of a Historically Widespread Pollinator Linked to Climate, Land Cover, and Pesticides," *Proceedings of the National Academy of Sciences* 120, no. 5 (January 23, 2023): e2211223120, https://doi.org/10.1073/pnas.2211223120.
5. Dacotah Melicher, Alex S. Torson, George D. Yocum, et al., "Metabolic and Transcriptomic Characterization of Summer and Winter Dormancy in the Solitary Bee, *Osmia lignaria*," *Insect Biochemistry and Molecular Biology* 166 (March 2024): 104074, https://doi.org/10.1016/j.ibmb.2024.104074.
6. Kim Kaplan, "Collecting a Library of Bee Genomes," USDA, October 1, 2024, www.ars.usda.gov/news-events/news/research-news/2022/collecting-a-library-of-bee-genomes/.

GLOSSARY

beehive Specific to honey bees, hives are typically artificial and frequently portable, so the beekeeper can place the hive where it is most wanted.

bee house An open-fronted container for multiple nesting tubes or trays; also called a nesting box.

bumble bee Members of the bee genus *Bombus*, which includes over 250 species worldwide (46 in North America). These social bees are easily identifiable by their fat, furry bodies.

chalkbrood A fungus (genus *Ascosphaera*) that proliferates rapidly through beehives and bee houses as tiny spores are ingested by larvae and spread to other areas of the hive or house, as well as back to plants, through contact with bee wings.

cocoon The grayish capsule spun by mason bee larvae that they hibernate in over the winter and hatch from in spring. Cocoons seem delicate but are surprisingly tough, designed to be waterproof and weather resistant.

colony collapse disorder (CCD) An event in a honey bee hive in which almost all the worker bees abandon the queen. It has been documented under a variety of names since the mid-1800s, but for most of that time, it was rare enough to not be a major source of concern to beekeepers. There has been a dramatic rise in the number of hives affected in the 21st century, causing the loss of between 30 and 50 percent of hives across North America.

community garden/orchard Patches of land typically owned by the local government and managed by the parks department; these may also be owned by nonprofit organizations. Volunteer gardeners sign up for garden space to care for and harvest from individually or to tend trees as part of a group effort and share in the harvest.

egg Laid one at a time by solitary queens and in large masses by social queens, eggs are the first stage of life in bee reproduction.

egg chamber For solitary bees, this includes an egg, a mass of pollen and nectar to feed the egg once it hatches, and a small amount of nesting material to separate the chambers.

frass The excrement of insects.

glyphosate A nonselective herbicide registered for use in the United States in 1974. It prevents plants from making specific proteins critical for their growth and is available in many forms, including solids or a dark liquid. There are more than 750 products containing glyphosate for sale in the United States, most notably Monsanto's Roundup.

hibernation For mason and leaf bees, a prolonged state of inactivity that lasts about nine months a year.

honey bee A social bee native to Europe but established in North America for centuries. This is the only species under threat from CCD.

Houdini fly A species of fruit fly that is a kleptoparasite. It does not attack mason bees directly but rather lays its eggs on the pollen meant for mason bee young.

larva (pl. larvae) What hatches from the egg laid by a queen, just a few days after the egg is laid. Larvae eat the pollen-and-nectar ball and spin the cocoons in which they grow into pupae.

leaf bee Also known as leafcutter bee or alfalfa leafcutter, a common solitary bee found throughout North America, most active during the summer months. The name is derived from the tiny pieces of leaf they collect for nesting material.

mason bee A solitary bee that nests in existing holes or cavities. There are more than 130 species of mason bees found in most North American states and provinces, the blue orchard mason bee being one of the better known. The term *mason* probably derives from the bees sealing each egg chamber with a nesting separating material.

meconium Metabolic waste produced by pupa, expelled by insects upon their emergence.

monodontomerus A parasitic wasp that deposits its eggs inside mason bee larva, ultimately killing the mason bee while it is still in the cocoon.

natural reed A family of plants that are tall and hollow and grow in wetlands and on floodplains. A common wild plant, they are also planted in beds to remove pollutants from lakes. Harvested by beekeepers for use as nesting tubes, they are also used for musical instruments, baskets, and traditional English thatched roofs.

nectar The sweet-smelling and tasting liquid secreted by flowers, nectar is combined with pollen to create a nourishing bee bread for developing bee larva—and other pollinators as well.

nesting box An open-fronted container for multiple nesting tubes or trays, also called a bee house.

nesting trays Easily cleanable, reusable wooden trays that are contoured so that, when stacked, they form tubes between them in which bees can nest. Taking them apart then gives gardeners easy access to harvest cocoons.

nesting tubes Tubes placed in bee houses and nesting boxes for cocoons to hatch from, and for mason and leaf bees to fill with egg chambers. They may be made of paper, cardboard, or lake-bed reeds.

nosema A disease, also called nosemosis, caused by a single-cell parasitic fungus that particularly affects honey bees. The spores are extraordinarily hard to kill. There are two identified types so far: *Nosema apis* and *Nosema ceranae. N. ceranae* was originally found in Taiwan but has spread rapidly through European honey bee populations in the 21st century.

ovipositor The tubular egg-laying organ of female insects.

parasitic wasp Any of more than 100,000 species of pollinating wasp of which most have evolved to prey on one specific species of insect (a small number can take advantage of multiple host insects). Mason bees and leaf bees each have a specific parasitic wasp that preys on them.

pheromone Scents that emanate from bodily fluids. Female bees use them to mark their nests and attract males.

pollen The yellow or golden powder found on the stamens of flowers. Mixed with nectar, it nourishes developing bee larva.

pollen mites Tiny insects that hitchhike to bee houses on the pollen carried by bees. In nesting tubes or trays, juvenile pollen mites look like fine-grained, bright orange sawdust.

pollination The process that fertilizes flowers, allowing them to mature into fruits. This can be accomplished by wind, an insect, a bird, or a mammal (including a human using delicate tools to hand-transfer pollen from one stamen to another).

pupa (pl. pupae) The final stage of metamorphosis before hatching. Once a larva has spun a cocoon, it pupates, and the pupa grows and hibernates until it hatches as an adult bee many months later.

queen A female bee capable of reproducing. While social bees have only one per colony, each solitary bee female is a queen.

scopa Any kind of anatomical structure used by nonparasitic bees to collect pollen. These include dense hairs on hind legs and pollen baskets, depending on the species.

social bees Bees that live in an organized family structure in groups numbering between 50 and 50,000 bees. There is only one queen and a clear division of labor among family members.

solitary bees Bees that live without an organized family structure but may live next to each other at close quarters. Every female is a queen and gathers food and nesting material for one egg at a time.

varroa mite A parasite that attacks both adult honey bees and the brood of young bees within a beehive. Its blood sucking in the brood results in adult bees that are weak or missing legs or wings.

wild bee A bee that lives without the benefit of human husbandry efforts. This can be either a social bee or a solitary bee. Depending on the species, wild bees can be attracted to gardens or infest a house.

yellowjacket The North American term for many kinds of wasps and also a name specific to a few species, such as eastern, prairie, southern, and western yellowjackets. They nest in the ground or in wood-frame buildings and defend their nests aggressively. At specific stages in development, they are strongly attracted to meat, which makes them a notable pest to people eating outdoors.

RESOURCES

ONLINE INFORMATION

American Community Garden Association
This organization builds community by increasing and enhancing community gardening across the United States and Canada.
www.communitygarden.org

Bat Conservation International
Active in the realms of bat education and conservation.
www.batcon.org

Bat World Sanctuary
A volunteer-supported indoor sanctuary for non-releasable bats that offers fascinating bat cams and information on white-nose syndrome.
https://batworld.org

Garden for Wildlife
In addition to selling many types of milkweed and other seeds for pollinator species, this National Wildlife Federation program offers steps to make your garden a Certified Wildlife Habitat.
https://gardenforwildlife.com

GardenWeb Forums
A longstanding set of user forums that supply answers on everything from organic gardening methods to pollinator-friendly techniques to recommended plants for your planting zone.
www.gardenweb.com

Grassland Heritage Foundation
Devoted to prairie study and preservation in northeastern Kansas.
www.grasslandheritage.org

The Great Sunflower Project
A massive citizen-science project that looks at the connection between flowers and a broad number of pollinators.
www.greatsunflower.org

Honey Bee Research Centre

A nonprofit based in Ontario, Canada, committed to scientific agricultural research in the area of pollinating insects and related materials and processes.
https://hbrc.ca

Monarch Joint Venture

A leader in conservation of the monarch butterfly, this national partnership works in collaboration to protect pollinators.
https://monarchjointventure.org

Monarch Watch

Among other monarch butterfly–focused efforts, this nonprofit oversees the collection and distribution of many species of milkweed.
https://monarchwatch.org

National Garden Clubs

Headquartered in St. Louis, Missouri, this organization provides educational opportunities, grants, and additional resources to individual and regional club members interested in an array of garden-focused topics.
https://gardenclub.org

Natural Resources Conservation Service

Formerly known as the US Soil Conservation Service, the NRCS, administered by the USDA, helps ranchers and farmers with the conservation of habitat on agricultural land by offering technical expertise, long-term easements, and solutions for farms of all sizes.
www.nrcs.usda.gov

North American Native Plant Society

Dedicating to preserving native plant habitat in wild areas and restoring indigenous plantings in urban and suburban communities.
https://nanps.org

Orchard Bee Association

A nonprofit, science-centered organization focused on mason bees.
www.orchardbee.org

Permies

An informative site with articles, videos, and a podcast on many topics related to permaculture and homesteading.
www.permies.com

Pollinator Partnership

Numerous programs are under the umbrella of this sizable public-private partnership. Canada's organization is related, but separate.
www.pollinator.org
https://pollinatorpartnership.ca

World Permaculture Day / Permaculture Week

Search for Permaculture Day and Week activities in your area or register your own event.
www.permacultureday.org

Xerces Society

A nonprofit organization that has worked for more than four decades to protect wildlife through the conservation of invertebrates and their habitats.
www.xerces.org

SOLITARY BEE SUPPLIES

Beediverse

Company founder Dr. Margriet Dogterom offers mason bee houses, nesting supplies, mason and leaf bee cocoons, and many educational accessories, including books, posters, and DVDs. While we don't endorse their products that include plastic components, the site is worth checking out.
https://beediverse.com

Best Bees

Provides urban solitary and hive beekeeping services for commercial, nonprofit, and occasional residential locations in 15 metro areas across the US.
https://bestbees.com

Crown Bees

Dave Hunter's product line offers complete supplies, including cocoons, for mason bee, leaf bee, and bumble beekeepers. Crown Bees' website features a downloadable resource guide, a cocoon buyback program, and links to a speakers bureau. Their free "Bee-Mail" newsletter is a regular source of timely tips.
https://crownbees.com

Rent Mason Bees

For those not able to commit to seasonal mason bee care, this company rents nesting blocks of about 50 cocoons. They also have a solitary bee rental program for farms with more than 100 acres (both are US only).
https://rentmasonbees.com

West Coast Seeds

In addition to an interesting line of vegetable and flower seeds, this company offers mason bee cocoons, several house designs, and mason bee mud.
www.westcoastseeds.com

SEED COMPANIES

Alliance of Native Seedkeepers

Prioritizing non-GMO (genetically modified organism), open-pollinated seeds and based in North Carolina, this small, worker-owned and Native-owned collective creates small, inexpensive seed packets well-suited to patio gardeners in many climates. Seeds are not limited to native varieties, but include a broad variety.
www.allianceofnativeseedkeepers.com

BFI Native Seeds

Selling both individual grass-seed types and mixes designed for highly specific western regions, this company is most useful when you wish to convert a large patch of land to native grasses.
www.bfinativeseeds.com

Canadian Organic Seed Company

The bee-friendly seeds they recommend are based on their own observation on nectar-rich plants their bees enjoy most. A welcome source of seeds for native plants across Canada and interesting heirloom vegetables.
https://certifiedseeds.ca

Eloheh Indigenous Center for Earth Justice

A regenerative, Native-owned teaching farm in Oregon, their seed selections include numerous North American native plants (ships only to US addresses).
www.elohehseeds.com

Outside Pride
A non-GMO seed company with an outstanding selection of clovers, with clear descriptions of each clover's native region and nice photos of what the plant looks like in bloom. Also a terrific array of North American native grass seeds.
www.outsidepride.com

Renee's Garden
An excellent non-GMO seed company that offers a good selection of heirloom vegetables and flowers, certified organic seeds, interesting hybrids, and open-pollinated varieties.
www.reneesgarden.com

Sistah Seeds
Based on a small farm in rural Pennsylvania, their mission is to "regenerate culturally-important varieties and seed-keeping traditions from the African Diaspora, while uplifting black seed stories and empowering aspiring black seed stewards." It's an excellent source of heirloom vegetables.
https://sistahseeds.com

Stover Seed
This century-old seed company is a member of the Pollinator Partnership that produces regional wildflower seed mixes.
https://shop.stoverseed.com

True Leaf Market
An independent, non-GMO seed company based in Utah. Their offerings include cover crops and heirlooms in amounts that suit both patio gardeners and commercial operations.
https://trueleafmarket.com

Uprising Seeds
A certified organic seed company based in Washington state that offers a terrific selection of pollinator-friendly herbs, vegetables, and flowers.
https://uprisingorganics.com

Vesey's Seeds
Operating from Prince Edward Island, Canada, since 1939, Vesey's offers organic and conventional seed, including some hard-to-find heirlooms. A small selection of homes for a variety of pollinators is also available.
www.veseys.com

SPECIALTY HONEY AND PLANT-BASED HONEY ALTERNATIVES

Bee Wild (LGBTQ-owned)
https://beewild.buzz

Capstone Honey (New Orleans nonprofit food resource)
www.capstone118.org

Detroit Hives (Black-owned)
https://detroithives.org

Ioway Bee Farm (Native-owned)
https://iowaybeefarm.com

Mellody (plant-based honey alternative)
https://mellodyfoods.com or https://crownbees.com

Register Family Farm (veteran-owned)
https://registerfamilyfarm.com

POLLINATOR TOURS AND SPECIALIZED HONEY BEE CLASSES

Astor Apiaries

New York–based honey collective that offers hive tours in the Compost Collective in Forest Hills, Queens, and at Green-Wood Cemetery in Sunset Park, Brooklyn.
https://astorapiaries.com/collections/hive-tours

BeeVangelists

Charlie Keonen offers small-format classes in and around his home base of Milwaukee, Wisconsin.
https://beevangelists.org

Euchee Butterfly Farm

This Native-led Oklahoma nonprofit's comprehensive tour includes a monarch butterfly farm, greenhouses, nature trails through a habitat restoration project, and a native seed bank with thousands of milkweed varieties.
www.nativebutterflies.org/tours

Half Mad Hives

Apiary in Philadelphia's Navy Yard offers small group and private hive tours that aim to help reduce the fear of bees.
www.halfmadhoney.com

NATIVE PLANT NURSERIES

Often, the best selection of native plants is available through your nearest native plant society, which typically operates at the state/provincial level and can be found by searching the internet under your state's/province's name and the words "native plant society." An alternative is to search the national native-plant nursery listing website Plantnative.org. We've supplied here a handful of nursery options to get you started.

Bowman's Hill Wildflower Preserve

A source for residents of Maryland, Delaware, New Jersey, and eastern Pennsylvania, the preserve hosts two native plant sales each year, offering more than 200 varieties of vines, ferns, shrubs, trees, and wildflowers, all of them grown in their nursery and not wild gathered.
https://bhwp.org

Mail Order Natives

The collection of native species at this central north Florida nursery includes perennials, interesting edibles, a special collection for butterfly larval needs, and a number of oaks, palms, and grasses. It's an excellent resource for the southeastern United States.
www.mailordernatives.com

Plants of the Southwest

Established in New Mexico in 1976, this nursery sells more than 400 varieties of native seeds that suit the dry climate of the Southwest. They'll ship the seeds but will refer you to a partner nursery for live plants. Their beautiful array of wildflowers proves that the desert can bloom like no other climate.
www.plantsofthesouthwest.com

Prairie Moon Nursery

A great resource in the Midwest, this nursery offers seeds and seed mixes for a broad array of habitats and special cases, including wetland restoration and monarch specialization, as well as bare-root plants that are never dug from the wild.
www.prairiemoon.com

Raintree Nursery

This Pacific Northwest nursery offers a broad selection of North and South American native vines, trees, tubers, and shrubs.
https://raintreenursery.com

HABITAT LAND TRUSTS

Alliance of Canadian Land Trusts/Alliance canadienne des organismes de conservation

Rather than functioning as one land trust, this organization connects many trusts working to preserve land within Canada, coordinating with Wildlife Habitat Canada to distribute federal dollars equitably and to share information and projects across provinces.
https://aclt-acoc.ca

American Farmland Trust

This organization was founded in 1980 and has since permanently preserved 6.8 million acres (2.8 million hectares) of American farmland through a tool known as conservation easements. They have helped guide 27 state farmland trust organizations as well as numerous trusts at more localized levels.
https://farmland.org

Humane Society of the United States Wildlife Land Trust

The mission of this trust is to "celebrate and protect wild animals by creating permanent sanctuaries, preserving and enhancing natural habitat, and confronting cruelty."
www.humanesociety.org/wildlife-land-trust

The Nature Conservancy

Active since 1951, this global nonprofit has protected an astonishing 125 million acres (51 million hectares) around the world, connecting their staff scientists with international partners to preserve and protect wild habitat, from coral reefs to rainforests to alpine meadows.
www.nature.org

Trust for Public Land

Founded in 1972, this trust has conserved about 4 million acres (1.6 hectares) with a focus on equity and climate resiliency. Many of their projects restore land to Native communities.
www.tpl.org

ADDITIONAL PHOTO CREDITS

Christopher L. Bonis: pages 94, 107, 158
Noah Emad/Shutterstock: page 137
Dave Hunter/Crown Bees: pages 20, 29, 62, 84
ifiStudio/Shutterstock: pages 9, 122
Jill Lightner: pages 7, 49, 87, 146
Lyudmila 2509/Shutterstock: page 75
Pollinator Partnership: page 19
Bryan Reynolds: pages 34, 50, 53, 95, 152, 154
Gina Lee Rodgers/Shutterstock: page 126
Theresa Singer: page 176
Barbara Smits/Shutterstock: page 141
Stock_studio/Shutterstock: page 71

INDEX

M

N

O

P

ABOUT THE AUTHORS

DAVE HUNTER began raising mason bees as a hobby in the early 1990s and this led him to create the Orchard Bee Association and to serve as its president for three years. In 2008, Dave founded Crown Bees, and their products have been available at nurseries, garden centers, and hardware stores for more than a decade. Today, Dave serves as an adviser on a multiyear USDA grant, the Integrated Crop Pollination Project, and he teams up with multiple government and academic researchers on mason bee studies. He regularly speaks on mason bee–related topics across the United States. Dave lives with his wife, Barb, in Woodinville, Washington. His passion is to create more food around the world by helping farmers and gardeners use the right bee on the right crop. Find out more at crownbees.com

JILL LIGHTNER is the author of *Scraps, Peels, and Stems: Recipes and Tips for Rethinking Food Waste at Home* (Skipstone, 2018) in addition to two other cookbooks and a recipe app. She edited two food publications and has written for many, winning a James Beard and a Gold Book Nautilus award. These days she contributes regularly to the *Seattle Times* and operates a Little Free Bakery box for her neighborhood. Her first direct connection to pollinators was as a toddler, when she survived sitting in a yellowjacket nest thanks to a combination of luck, calm family members, and ice cream. Learn more about her at Jilllightner.com.

ABOUT SKIPSTONE

Skipstone is an imprint of independent, nonprofit publisher Mountaineers Books. It features thematically related titles that promote a deeper connection to our natural world through sustainable practice and backyard activism. Our readers live smart, play well, and typically engage with the community around them. Skipstone guides explore healthy lifestyles and how an outdoor life relates to the well-being of our planet, as well as of our own neighborhoods. Sustainable foods and gardens; healthful living; realistic and doable conservation at home; modern aspirations for community—Skipstone tries to address such topics in ways that emphasize active living, local and grassroots practices, and a small footprint.

Our hope is that Skipstone books will inspire you to effect change without losing your sense of humor, to celebrate the freedom and generosity of a life outdoors, and to move forward with gentle leaps or breathtaking bounds.

All of our publications, as part of our 501(c)(3) nonprofit program, are made possible through the generosity of donors and through sales of 700 titles on outdoor recreation, sustainable lifestyle, and conservation. To donate, purchase books, or learn more, visit us online:

SKIPSTONE

LIVE LIFE

MAKE RIPPLES

www.skipstonebooks.org
www.mountaineersbooks.org